Caddos, Cotton and Cowboys

Essays on Arlington

By

O.K. Carter

Frank — Enjoy arlington's
colorful history — The Gilstraps
are a big name here!

O.K. Carter

Arlington Woman's Club
AWC Crest designed by Beth Anderson and Julie Jones

Published by Arlington Woman's Club
Arlington, Texas
The author of this book has donated proceeds of
its sale to the Arlington Woman's Club.

About the Cover

Artist Irene Glass has recreated a scene typical of the late 1800s, when
the big industry in Arlington was cotton ginning. Farmers from
throughout the region brought their cotton to Arlington for processing
and bailing. Then it was sold to buyers, who hauled it to the Main Street
station and packed it aboard trains headed for big cloth mills back east
and in Europe.

Cover design by Connie Ruff

Table of Contents

O.K. Carter

Author's Note

This book has its origins in a promise made to Arista Joyner in the final days of her remarkable life. *Arlington Citizen-Journal* Editor Sharon Cox and I had edited and supervised publication of the second edition of Joyner's book, *Arlington, Texas: Birthplace of the Metroplex,* which essentially stopped at 1910. Joyner—a journalist, painter, poet and arts advocate—extracted what amounted to a deathbed promise that I would write a much more complete history of the city.

Flash forward to a meeting with the Arlington Woman's Club a few years later and a casual suggestion that perhaps club members would be interested in designing, editing and publishing such a book. They were, and this book is dedicated to them with profound appreciation but also with this acknowledgement: OK, Arista, here it is.

I am not a historian. I'm a journalist, which means that this book will not be laced with source footnotes. *Caddos, Cotton and Cowboys: Essays on Arlington* is an attempt to reflect a profile of a place I've been covering in either the *Arlington Citizen-Journal* or *Fort Worth Star-Telegram* for more than three decades. Arlington itself is the primary character. Every community, of course, has a unique history and flavor. But in terms of urban development Arlington stands alone as the only municipality among the nation's fifty most populous cities to prosper in the midst of—what turned out to be the magic middle—two giant and competing cities, Dallas and Fort Worth. That story, stretching across

5

more than 160 years, is told here in as succinct a manner as I could manage.

I owe a great many people and institutions. I have spent many hours in the archives of the *Star-Telegram* and *Citizen-Journal*, both of which are maintained in Special Collections at the University of Texas at Arlington. I have borrowed extensively and shamelessly from those archives. They are the *Rosetta's Stone* of this modest collection of essays. Without Joyner's book I would never have become interested or so vested in Arlington's history. I consider myself a story teller but also a story listener. In particular I have listened to stories of old Arlington from a gang of accomplished raconteurs: Tom Vandergriff, Richard Greene, Dorothy Rencurrel, Geraldine Mills, Martha Martin, Bill Bardin, George and Charles Hawkes, Wendell Nedderman, Bryan Cotter, Eleanor Martin, Staley McBrayer, Paul Geisel, Dick Malec, Kris Landrith, Randy Ford, "Bubba" Welch, Harold Patterson, Barton Thompson, Jerry Jordan, Dottie Lynn, O.L. Watson, Emory and Dorothy Estes, Gary Cartwright, Jerre Todd, Allan Saxe, Carl Pointer, Donna Darovich, Sue Durbec and many others.

No one knew more about Arlington history from 1940 on than town Fire Marshal J.W. Dunlop, and for many years he was my go-to guy, a vast repository of tiny details (and yes, sometimes juicy gossip). Many of these old friends are no longer with us, but they live on as community legends. If I had known I was going to write a book and that they were not going to be eternally present, I would have recorded them all.

The writer of a book like this inevitably ends up reading as much as writing. I particularly want to thank Allan Saxe, who's *Politics of Arlington, Texas* has saved me from a great deal of tedious research.

Donna Darovich's *Arlington: Center Stage in the Metroplex* was very useful, as was Gerald Saxon's definitive book of UT Arlington history, *Transitions: A Centennial History of The University of Texas at Arlington.*

Phyllis Forehand's master's degree thesis, *The History of the Arlington Citizen-Journal*, is both a terrific history of early media in newspapers and a reflection on more than 80 years of media coverage of the city.

I have already mentioned Arista Joyner and her *Arlington, Texas: Birthplace of the Metroplex*, but the importance of her work and research to this book cannot be overstated.

The following is a partial list of additional books, periodicals, and authors to which and whom I owe a debt of gratitude:

Middleton Tate Johnson: The Father of Tarrant County, Katherine Allred

History of Tarrant County from its Beginning until 1875, Verna Berrong

Berachah: The Life and Works of J.T. and Maggie Upchurch, Dorothy Upchurch Betts

The History of Arlington Schools, Council of PTAs

Indian Fighting On the Texas Frontier, John Elkins

Lone Star: A History of Texas and the Texans, T.R. Fehrenbach

The Cast Iron Forest: A Natural and Cultural History of the North American Cross Timbers, Richard Francaviglia

Fort Worth, A Frontier Triumph, Julia Garrett

Wild West Days of Arlington, Texas, Carol Henning

Texas Monthly, Gary Cartwright

The New Handbook of Texas

The Bankhead Highway and Its Evolution through Arlington, Texas, Stephen Barnes

History of Arlington, Texas, Web Rose, S.R. Yates and P.A. Watson

How Fort Worth Became the Texasmost City, Leonard Sanders

Gamblers and Gangsters, Ann Arnold

Fort Worth and Tarrant County: A Historical Guide, Ruby Schmidt and others.

Thanks as well to Laura Lace who got the project rolling, the "minder" Mary Laport who kept us on track and gifted artist and illustrator Irene Glass. Also, my gratitude goes to Sue Stevens Durbec and Connie Ruff for taking care of publishing and design details and for being stalwart friends.

Over the years, dozens of people volunteered historical information. Many gave interviews or provided anecdotes. I thank them and hope that something of what they said ended up in the book. If I have forgotten anyone or neglected to credit a source—and most certainly I have—then I apologize. History should be passed on from generation to generation, and in that spirit I encourage the full use of any material within these pages by anyone in the future—with or without a footnote credit.

Chapter 1 – Overview

Arlington has led the life of a municipal chameleon, an ever-adapting changeling that began its existence as a struggling, besieged, ramshackle Republic of Texas fort on a meandering oxbow lake by an oft-flooded Trinity River, but which evolved into the largest mid-city in America and a showplace for events like the World Series and Super Bowl.

Its story, even by epic Texas standards where the tall tale arrives as standard fare, qualifies as a remarkable tale of persistence, skill, luck, leadership, changing identity and an entrepreneurial flexibility that in the ever-revealing glow of historical hindsight qualifies as nothing less than astonishing. It is a geography where prairie and woodlands collide—a place where weather ranges from tropical to blizzard and from monsoonal to drought, but is mostly temperate. Once described as the place where East meets West, Arlington's history includes battles between Texas Rangers and Comanches, vast herds of grazing bison, westward expansion, an urban gas drilling bonanza, train crashes, six-shooter gun fights in the middle of downtown, saloons and cotton gins, slavery, high-stakes gambling, hard-scrabble farming, temperance and prohibition, industry, tourism and the not-always-welcome embrace of never-ending capitalistic competition. It has not always been pretty; the city has always been a gritty, make-it-happen kind of place.

Arlington's identity has been ever-shifting. In the 1940s and early 1950s, many of its residents would have described it as almost classic Mayberry—an idyllic small town with drug stores, movie houses, a pool hall and haberdashers downtown. In earlier times it was famous for mineral waters, gambling and gangsters in perpetual conflict with Bible thumping Baptists and Texas Rangers. It was also a refuge for unwed mothers, an incubator for industry and commerce and the nation's fastest growing municipality, as well as a college town. Over decades it evolved into the poster city for a trend that reshaped America—the surge to suburbia from farms, ranches and central cities.

Today, people around the world know about Arlington for other reasons. The hundreds of millions who watched the 2011 Super Bowl were told in no uncertain terms that the game was coming to them from the "Dallas" Cowboys stadium in Arlington, Texas.

Cowboys Stadium

They received the same message again when the Arlington-based Texas Rangers took on the San Francisco Giants in the 2010 World Series and then made a repeat appearance against the St. Louis Cardinals in the 2011 series.

Rangers Ball Park in Arlington

Today's brand or image for Arlington tends to be about roller coasters, Major League Baseball and NFL football, but it is also one of the nation's 50 most populous cities. As of the 2010 census, more than 366,000 people lived in Arlington, an endorsement for quality of life in one of the most conveniently located, amenity-rich municipal environments in the nation. It is a city that has come a very long way from its early origins as a rag-tag fort and a 5-minute train stop town.

How did it come so far? How did it change so very much? How could it be so flexible; so very adaptable? Before Arlington began its transition into one of America's largest cities, pundits in Dallas and Fort Worth often described the city as the "hyphen" between Dallas and Fort Worth. This comparison likening the city to a minor bit of punctuation qualifies as an understatement and also is indicative of the once dismissive tendencies toward Arlington from leadership in the larger cities of Dallas and Fort Worth. Indeed, perhaps because the word "Arlington" takes considerable map space, early maps of the area sometimes didn't show the city at all, much to the consternation of the local chamber of commerce and community leadership. Today, however, Arlington often receives more attention in national and international news than its larger sister communities to the east and west.

That "hyphen" business does, in fact, offer a clue to two of the three characteristics that have been most dominant in shaping and growing Arlington since the city was incorporated in1884.

The first of those is almost so simple that it is accepted as a given: It is its location almost precisely mid-way between Dallas and Fort Worth and also almost geographically in the center of the vast Metroplex, itself more populous than more than 25 states. This highly accessible and convenient location is an almost lucky accident that began with the desire by the Texas and Pacific Railroad to have a railroad stop midway between Dallas and Fort Worth. Originally surveyed in 1876, Arlington as a formally organized and incorporated city (1884) owes its very existence to this decision and has been profiting from it for more than a century.

The second of those characteristics is that life as a mid-city, bracketed by two much larger municipalities, meant that those cities— Dallas and Fort Worth—had both political and economic clout far exceeding that of Arlington. It would have been easy enough for Arlington's leadership to accept the "hyphen" and "suburb" labels conferred upon it by its larger neighbors, but this did not occur. Instead, particularly from the 1950s on, Arlington's elective and community leadership recognized the imbalances and became both increasingly competitive and, for lack of a better word, "entrepreneurial" in seeking new commercial and residential growth. Most certainly the city's magic-middle location helped, but location by itself would not have been enough to attract a Great Southwest Industrial District, a GM plant, thousands of new homes and residents, the Six Flags Over Texas Amusement Park and—more recently—the Texas Rangers Baseball Team and Dallas Cowboys. Competition both makes and breaks cities. In Arlington's case, constant competition and early successes in attracting major new developments, like GM, both showed a "can do" underdog spirit and a zeal for competitive innovation that paid off in new economic development and in attracting new residents.

The third factor is too often overlooked in a community: There is no substitute, none at all, for being a college town. What now is the University of Texas at Arlington (UTA) has been in place since before 1900.

University of Texas Arlington

A college is an economic development entity in itself but more importantly outshines any single other type of organization in improving a community's quality of life. A college attracts students who become well-educated future citizens. It brings in faculty who are experts in engineering, science, literature, the arts and myriad other disciplines. Colleges attract new residents and new businesses and are the single most important component of appealing to younger, more entrepreneurial, well-educated residents, who over time inherit the mantle of leadership in business, culture, social services and politics. That Arlington has UTA—and now Tarrant County College and Arlington Baptist College—represents an advantage that cannot be overvalued.

Many years ago, Arlington's then-Mayor Tom Vandergriff was asked what the key was to Arlington growing so rapidly. Indeed, for the first three decades after 1950, Arlington was the fastest growing city in the nation.

Vandergriff pondered the question: "There are three reasons," he said, half-jokingly. "Location, location and location."

If not for modesty the now-deceased mayor could have just as well added, "….and Vandergriff, Vandergriff and Vandergriff," so great was his influence in the quarter-century of his administration. But more about the former mayor later.

Mayor Tom Vandergriff

Arlington is almost equidistant from the downtowns of both Big D, that's Dallas and Cowtown, that's Fort Worth, though Fort Worthians (some of them anyway) have been trying to distance themselves from the town's Old West brand for a while. Regardless, from the middle of Arlington to the downtowns of either of its colossal neighbors (both are in the nation's 20 largest cities), it is about 16 miles on either of the town's two interstates. At the customary Texas cruising speed of 75 to 80 mph in the slow lane that means it's a 10 to 15 minute drive-time trip. Texas is big and those who want to get somewhere in a reasonable time, put the pedal to the metal. Not that there's an option to the auto. Of the nation's 100 most populous cities, only Arlington offers neither rail of bus transit; voters having turned down development of mass transit three times.

"I'm beginning to think that residents don't like it," former Mayor Richard Greene joked after the third such transit election, none of which came close to getting passed by the electorate. The town just likes autos, with the average household having 2.1 vehicles.

The first-time visitor to Arlington often has difficulties tuning in to a realistic sense of place and community. There's just too much visual distraction, though seeing isn't necessarily always believing. Skylines dominate the persona of some cities, while others have seaport vistas, mountain ranges or wide rivers as visual themes. But approach Arlington from the usual access on either I-20 or I-30—the two interstates that serve as cash flowing economic Mississippi rivers for the town—and a colossus appearing not unlike a galactic starship dominates the prairie vista.

This looming "Holy smokes, what is that?" architectural what-do-you-call-it is the Cowboys Stadium, the planet's largest domed structure, sprawling across three million square feet and escalating 20 stories high. Wags have nicknamed the $1.2 billion indoor stadium as "Jerry World," a reference to Cowboys owner Jerry Jones. Though it did not occur without assistance, Arlington voters liked the stadium idea back in 2004 when 55.2 percent in a local-election, with an 11,000 record voters, agreed to finance $325 million worth of what was supposed to be a $650 million stadium. Once again Arlington's finely-honed competitive tendencies prevailed, with the city virtually snagging the Cowboys' project from Dallas' apparently complacent grip.

Arlingtonites ended up receiving considerably more than their money's worth because the structure ultimately cost about $1.2 billion, with the taxpayer share staying at $325 million. That's not counting assorted nearby infrastructure improvements like the revamped I-30 interchanges; so call it $450 million from the public pocket, with a substantial chunk coming from other governmental entities like the county and state. Though governmental investment in private enterprise has its critics, voters supported it. The Cowboys are now considered the most valuable sports franchise on planet Earth.

The stadium looms miles away as a monumental gleaming silver disk, so overwhelming and dominating a presence on the banks of pastoral Johnson Creek that the casual visitor tends to think of tourism and visitation to be what the city is all about. Pilots say the stadium can be easily distinguished at 20,000 feet. This change in city brand is not an easy concept to absorb because prior to the presence of the stadium Arlington was mostly known for baseball and roller coasters. The visitation business is big in today's Arlington. Huge. Colossal.

Cowboys Stadium

As previously noted, Major League Baseball's Texas Rangers also call Arlington home. The team has been less than successful for most of its history but is fresh off a town-frenzying but ultimately losing second

World Series run. It's a team run and partially owned by the legendary Hall of Fame fire-baller Nolan Ryan. The ballpark resides just down the street two blocks from the Cowboys. The Rangers' charming but modest 49,000-seat throwback-style ballpark, engineered by former president and Texas Governor George Bush before he was either, is clearly now dwarfed by the newly arrived Cowboys.

The same is true for the nearby Six Flags Over Texas Amusement Park, the original mother-ship for the Six Flags Amusement Park chain of parks. Once upon a time, the visage of screaming kids on the parachute drop or riding roller coasters hands-free was the image visitors took away as being all about Arlington. The kids still scream at Six Flags roller coasters, and at a giant water park called Hurricane Harbor on I-30 across from Six Flags. But it's near-impossible for newcomers to take their eyes off that golly-gee-whiz one big whopper of a quarter-mile long stadium surrounding a couple of goal posts.

The appeal of the attractions is evident. Arlington hosts the aforementioned millions of visitors annually, most showing up for a few hours and some staying overnight. Only the Alamo tops Six Flags in Lone Star state annual visitors, though the Alamo has an advantage. It's free. The cost of an adult ducat to Six Flags was about $35 in 2011, not bad for a day's entertainment compared to the average price of a Cowboys' ticket $160; the highest in the NFL. Entry to the world's largest and most expensive arena doesn't come cheap. Then again it was near impossible to buy a Super Bowl ticket at the stadium in 2011 for less than $1,000, and that was in the cheap seats.

But it would be a mistake to decide that tourism is what the city is all about. Lots of people opt to live here for reasons that have nothing to do with Jerry Jones or Nolan Ryan, roller coasters or water slides. Here are some quick facts: Though in fact the city ranks among the country's 50 most populous cities, it "plays" like a much smaller city. The 2010 census count of 365,438 placed it as 49th, and more people have residential addresses here than, say, St. Louis or Pittsburgh. Perhaps astonishingly, it has a smidge more population than Miami, but the Texas town's sprawling near-100 square miles just doesn't look the part.

North Texas is proud of its growth, so much so that it has dubbed itself the "Metroplex." If the name seems grandiosely similar to Metropolis of Superman fame, the resemblance is probably not coincidental. Texans like to exercise hyperbole. Looking for brags is a state genetic characteristic that trickles down to municipalities. Or maybe gushes down. Arlington and neighboring Grand Prairie have been known to quarrel over which of the cities resides in the exact middle of the Metroplex, geographically speaking. The answer is that they're both close enough so that it doesn't matter.

The reality about Arlington is that even though it has been around in one form or another since before 1850, it's mostly a new kind of place, the operant word being "mostly." Though the 2012 North Texas Council of Governments' estimate of population was almost 370,000, Arlington had only 7,800 residents back in 1950. Considering the town was incorporated in 1884 and existed as a Texas frontier outpost and village since about 1847, this reflects a not-so-hardy pastoral growth pattern for roughly a century. That's plenty of time for a town to grow a few ghosts, at least metaphorically. Though no doubt there are hordes of ghosts along the city's two interstates, a consequence of the frequently fatal pedal-to-the-metal mindset, the best way to get a sense of the old ghosts would be to cruise into Arlington at a sensible 40 mph on old Highway 80, Division Street, preferably from east to west, the same general directional tendency with which Texas was occupied by invading Anglos.

There is history here. At last count, Arlington boasted of almost 70 historical markers. There's a marker for old Bird's Fort, for instance, the first attempt to settle the area, "first attempt" not counting American Indians like the Caddos, who were farming, gathering and hunting in this part of the world hundreds and thousands of years ago. Several would-be settlers are buried near Bird's Fort, their graves long erased by occasionally surly Trinity River floods. Surely there are ghosts there.

And, though it's tucked away on a side street half a block off Division, there's a marker for what used to be Arlington Downs as well. If a ghost was actually around, the first spiritual manifestation on a Division Street historical cruise would probably be close to a marker eulogizing W.T. Waggoner, whose obituary proclaimed him to be the richest man west of the Mississippi.

Waggoner built a 25,000-seat horse racing track called Arlington Downs in 1929, and then persuaded the Texas Legislature to legalize pari-mutuel betting. Will Rogers and a future vice president, John Nance Garner, and a host of other celebrities showed up to wager on the daily double. The track boomed but its protector, Waggoner, had a stroke and died in the early 1930s. Without him around, the legislature bowed to both the pressures of preachers and the Great Depression to shut it down. Waggoner loved the ponies, particularly thoroughbreds, and it was said that his favorite phrase was "They're off!" Before the track was finally demolished, it evolved into a noisy auto racing track that captured at least an asterisk in movie lore: Clark Gable and Barbara Stanwyck used the track for a portion of their 1950's "B" movie, "To Please a Lady." It did not make the Academy Award nomination list but nevertheless remains Arlington's favorite movie.

Perhaps places have ghosts as well. The old downtown, the most prominent feature of which was a mineral well originally surrounded by five cotton gins, has disappeared. So have half a dozen saloons that were zapped by municipal prohibition before the nation jumped on the same bandwagon. Arlington pioneers drilled the mineral well in the middle of the town's most prominent intersection as a community amenity, planning for potable water. What they got was heavily mineralized water under so much pressure that 50,000 gallons a day flowed for years messily down Center Street, eventually evaporating and leaving a ghostly white film. Arlington crystals, sort of an Epson salt, were distilled from the concoction, once serving as a staple on medicine shelves. But no more.

Arlington Mineral Well

One of the old downtown movie theaters is gone, and the other now hosts Country Western weekend performances, interrupted periodically by concerts of the Arlington Symphony. Arlington's cultural tendencies tend to be liberally inclusive. Buildings, if they survive, get recycled. The old J.C. Penney's on Main Street is now The Arlington Museum of Art. The Kier lumberyard now houses Theatre Arlington, the community's cultural flagship. There's still a prominent bump under the intersection of Center and Main streets, or least where Main Street was before the city put a looping curl in it to make way for more parking at City Hall. Supposedly the bump covers the old wellhead and still connects to the mineral-laced water. Presumably it's still the same nasty stuff that was so vile that not even horses or pigs would drink it.

Though some old timers joke that Arlington was created by Presbyterians in search of a railroad, it was the Methodists who showed up first in the new town, quickly organizing in Shultz's Lumberyard in 1877, then setting up shop to stay. They're still there and prospering at the corner of Center and Abram streets, the massive Methodist structure book-ended downtown by an even more massive First Baptist complex three short blocks south. The big Baptist church organized a year earlier in Johnson Station but—like others of their church brethren—decided to migrate to this new Arlington place.

Where does the name "Arlington" originate? Start with John Bennett, appointed the Duke of Harlington, an area near London. But a cleric's error dubbed him the Duke of Arlington, inadvertently dropping the "H." Arlington, Vermont, and then Arlington, Virginia, were named in the duke's honor during the country's colonial era. Everything from there, one way or another, is a spinoff. The census says this country now has 16 cities called Arlington; 19 if both Arlington Heights and one Upper Arlington are included. The smallest is Arlington, Indiana, population 500 and slipping.

What is now Arlington, Texas, is the largest of "the Arlingtons" in both population and land area. But its population in 1876 was officially zero. The railroad, having completed a survey of what was then a half-mile square bit of prairie with no name, left the actual naming of the city to the swiftly arriving townspeople, two of the most prominent being newly anointed Postmaster James Ditto and Presbyterian minister-knife maker-surveyor Andrew Hayter.

The two picked the name "Arlington," allegedly as a roundabout way of honoring Confederate commanding General Robert E. Lee, whose home in Arlington, Virginia, was also called Arlington House. The town formally incorporated as exactly that in 1884. By then, other small nearby communities, Hayterville and Johnson Station, had folded up and their populations moved to the new-fangled Arlington place. By 1884 the emerging village already had an estimated 500 residents and was becoming a center for cotton farming and shipping.

Follow Center Street a half-block further south of the old mineral well and there's a longer, more linear bump on Abram Street outside City Hall. This middle-of-the road elevation is said to be covering the last remaining rails of the long-defunct Interurban electric trolley system that once ran from Dallas to Fort Worth. The Interurban ran from 1902 until 1937, turning out to be the city's last vestige of mass transit. The city used the trolley's excess electric power at night. Most of the Interurban rails were eventually ripped out to feed the war machine of World War II, melted and cast into battleships, mortars and fighter planes.

There's a reminder of the consequences of war on the lawn of the downtown library on Center Street, a memorial to Arlington Medal of Honor winner Col. Neel Kearby. The World War II ace shot down 22 Japanese planes with a probable score of seven more. He was brought down himself over New Guinea near Wewak and his body not recovered until after the war. The library memorial isn't far from his childhood home. His ghost may not reside here—he was a warrior of the skies after all—but the memory of the colonel and his flying machine definitely haunts this place.

City Hall across the street has its own historical marker as well, though it's more of a historical overview of general municipal creation. The back of City Hall, which everybody uses as the main entrance, looks out over what used to be the T&P Railroad station, evidence of which is now just a low loading ramp. If ghosts are anywhere in town, they're here. Though not a traditional Wild West sort of place, on Christmas Eve of 1892 it was here, 75 yards away from what is now City Hall, where J.H. Hargrove of Bowie showed up on the train in the company of his two sons, George and Walker, to iron out a dispute over a livestock deal with Arlington's Harvey Spears.

The discussion quickly evolved into a gunfight that left Spears, his friend "Poker" Bill Smith, the elder Hargrove and his son George all dead, along with the horse of a passing cowboy, the horse mowed down in the crossfire. The sole survivor, Walker Hargrove, eventually died in yet another gunfight in a Fort Worth saloon. Locals took up a collection for the cowboy, buying him another horse. The cowboy promptly decided to move on to less hazardous areas.

Inexplicably, there's no historical marker for the gunfight, nor does any marker note that it was here on this train that hundreds of young women, typically cast out homeless and in various stages of unwed pregnancy showed up. They then walked a mile to the nearby Berachah Industrial Home for the Redemption of Erring Girls, there to eventually bear their children and learn a trade.

Berachah Home

Nazarene Minister W.T. Upchurch or his wife or daughter operated the home from 1903 until it closed in 1942. The only remembrance of the home that survives is a small cemetery in Doug Russell Park on the UT Arlington campus. The smallish cemetery contains fewer than a hundred graves, the remains of mostly infants that died from assorted ailments, including a flu epidemic.

Texas Monthly writer Gary Cartwright grew up in Arlington, often using the popular magazine's pages to woefully chronicle the city's departure from his nostalgic version of "Our Town." Cartwright moved away in 1952. So his vision of the city is really about a city that exists only in memories. Here's his recollection of the Top O'Hill borrowed from his 2004 Texas Monthly article.

"Owned by gambler-entrepreneur Fred Browning, Top O'Hill Terrace included a casino that pulled down $250,000 on weekends, a ballroom where performers like Jimmy Dorsey entertained, a brothel, a tea garden, and several stables,"

Top O'Hill Terrace

Cartwright wrote. "Behind the casino walls was a warren of secret rooms and passageways. An underground escape tunnel led to the garden, where the likes of John Wayne, Howard Hughes, Joe Louis, Lana Turner, Will Rogers, Bonnie Parker and Clyde Barrow could pretend to be sipping tea whenever the joint got raided. The stone guardhouse at the entrance is still visible from Division Street. My dad told me that the manicured grounds were patrolled by men with machine guns and attack dogs wearing spiked collars. Led by the legendary Captain M. T. "Lone Wolf" Gonzaullas, the Texas Rangers raided Top O'Hill Terrace in 1947, encouraged, perhaps, by the firebrand pastor of Fort Worth's First Baptist Church, J. Frank Norris. His sanctimonious radio sermons drove Granny nuts."

Despite the clear violation of any number of state and local laws, the casino lasted 20 years. In one of those peculiar quirks of happenstance or perhaps Divine intervention, the property was eventually purchased by the Rev. Norris' Fort Worth church and converted to a college. An associated entity on the campus prepares missionaries for their duties throughout the world. It's Norris' statue that visitors see when entering the college grounds instead of owner Fred Browning or his partner, the equally legendary Benny "Cowboy" Binion. Binion eventually would become the creator of the Horseshoe in Las Vegas, funded by profits from the Arlington casino operation. For a while the casino brothel served as the Arlington Baptist College girls' dorm before it was eventually torn down. History can be quirky.

History seems to dote on tragedies over triumphs. In March 1885, Texas and Pacific Railroad Engine No. 642 derailed on the Village Creek Bridge, which had been weakened by flooding. Fireman J.C. Habeck was killed and several others injured. That would have been disaster enough but despite the best efforts of townspeople, the engine slowly sank deeper into the sand and mud until it was apparent it couldn't be saved. It remains embedded there today, with a strongbox that was never recovered despite an enthusiastic search by Arlington residents and gawkers from all over the region. Worse yet, the loss proved to be very bad news for the financially troubled T&P, which ended up filing for bankruptcy and falling into receivership, taking years to recover. History has both triumphs and victories.

First Downtown Arlington

New as Arlington is, it's also old—really older than either Fort Worth or Dallas—and with an abundance of its own history, some of it sentimental, some sad, some happy and sometimes savage. There are those, like hometown writer Cartwright, who would have preferred that Arlington stay as it was.

"It was a place where old men gathered and chewed tobacco and cussed Eleanor Roosevelt and played moon and watched the world go around," Cartwright wrote of the pre-1950 Arlington he so fondly recalls.

It is no doubt good to keep such memories. History is, after all, a critical component of sense of place. But there's also this reality: People really do vote with their feet, which in translation means they go where the opportunities are. It took Arlington a century to grow to 7,800 people. And then it became the quintessential suburban escape valve. A place where hundreds of thousands of people chose to live and work—or maybe commute to work or to attend college. Someday, those people will be as nostalgic for the Arlington of today as Cartwright is for his hometown of another era. The new downtown that is emerging this decade will not be like that of 1950. It will be new. And exciting to watch unfold.

But this book is not about the future. It is about the past and a colorful history, much of which—as the pages ahead unfold will demonstrate—is very unique indeed.

Chapter 2 – Cretaceous to Native Americans

Given enough time—say a few million years here and there—and every neighborhood changes. Sometimes it only takes a walk with an observant child to illustrate this phenomenon. And so it was on the unseasonably balmy January day in 2003 when Art Sahlstein took his 7-year-old daughter, Olivia, for a modest hike along the Trinity River in an as-yet-undeveloped section of northern Arlington.

Sahlstein calls such outings "prayer walks," but Olivia tends to be more about being in touch with Mother Nature, which is why she saw something strange in the earth. She ran to it.

"Olivia reached down and pulled a vertebra directly out of the ground," Sahlstein said. "She said, 'This is a dinosaur bone.'"

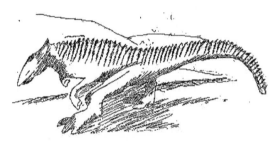

And so it was. Olivia Sahlstein was not the first person to see that the erosion along the creek area leading to the Trinity River revealed an unusual number of very odd looking fossilized remains. Area residents Bill Walker and Phil Kirchhoff also had spotted similar clues that pointed to the area being something of a paleontological twilight zone. That's "twilight" because the discovery turned out to be the most important discovery in this region in regard to finding rare fossils from the Mid-Cretaceous Period. The Mid-Cretaceous Period takes place before the more well-known Cretaceous era populated by the likes of Triceratops or T. Rex a mere 65 million years ago.

Southern Methodist University's Louis Jacobs, author of the book "Lone Star Dinosaurs," says this particular 2,200-acre swath of mixed prairie and trees was, 95 million to 119 million years ago, part of a flat shelf in an ancient tropical and salty ocean.

"Arlington was the Galveston or the Mississippi Delta of the Cretaceous," said Derek Main, then a University of Texas at Arlington doctoral student and dig supervisor. "More than half of Texas (including what is now Arlington depending on the time frame) was under water."

Long-time Arlington Realtor Gloria Van Zandt, herself something of a local historian, often made note of this, jokingly, in delivering sales pitches.

"What we have here in Arlington is beachfront property," she would tell prospective home buyers. "It's just been a while since the tide has come in."

Since the discovery of that solitary "dinosaur bone," UTA researchers at what is now labeled the Arlington Archosaur Site have been conducting extensive digs. They have unveiled a kind of time-machine revelation of what this particular Arlington neighborhood was once like. The word "Archosaur" covers the ruling reptiles of the era, that being dinosaurs and crocodiles.

Think of that old Arlington neighborhood as it would have been then: a Florida Keys-like ocean edge with mangrove trees along a swampy plain where fresh water emptied into the sea. Herbivorous dinosaurs—plant eaters—may have splashed in the shallows and muddy edges, taking care to avoid giant crocodiles, some exceeding 20 feet in length. Turtles, sharks and lungfish swam in the water. It was a harsh world also populated by meat-eating theropods, another type of dinosaur. Researchers at the Archosaur Site, helped by a steadily growing number of volunteers, have already unearthed remnants of giant crocodiles that appear to be a type previously unknown. There's also a new species of lungfish—a type of fish with both gills and lungs—and what could well turn out to be a new variety of Protohadros, a duck-billed dinosaur considered to be something of a missing link in dinosaur evolution. One dig area contains so many crocodile remains it has been dubbed "Crocorama," the major find being a crocodile of such massive size the assumption would be that it was king or queen of the pond. That's "almost king" because something, either another creature or a fluke of nature did, after all, manage to put an end to the crocodile's life. Clearly, Arlington was once a very tough tooth-and-claw neighborhood.

The excavations were scheduled to conclude in 2012 because the area, the last large undeveloped section of Arlington, was planned to become a mixed use river-lands community called Viridian, a future home to 20,000 new residents.

The Arlington site rests atop the Woodbine Formation, also known as the Eastern Cross Timbers, roughly the ancient oceanic beach. Its sand dune hills—don't forget that it began as a beach—are hospitable to scrubby growths of post oaks and blackjack oaks. Dig Supervisor Main likes to remind local residents that they all live atop fossil-rich rock. "People forget what they live on," he points out.

In short, kick over any rock around Arlington, and it's quite possible that a fossilized shark tooth will be imbedded in it. Or maybe the skull of a duck-billed dinosaur.

There's another powerful reminder of this "we forget what they live on" oddity as well, dotting empty landscapes throughout Arlington and this particular region. In recent years, gas wells have popped up by the thousands in the region. Driven by the economics of higher natural gas prices, the wells were made possible through a combination of quickly advancing slant well technology—drilling vertically to gas-rich deposits and horizontally through the deposit itself—as well as more efficient hydraulic fracturing techniques, a way to force gas loose from deep underground.

Those wells tap into the Barnett Shale, which in this 17-county region can be anywhere from 3,000 to 8,000 feet below. How did it get there? For several million years starting about 323 million years ago—the Mississippian Age---the area was under a shallow sea. The bottom steadily received and compressed organic materials, a deepening soup that could be thousands of feet thick and made up of eons of carbon-based life and death struggles in the sea.

The ocean eventually receded, but this was also a time of what might be described, with considerable simplification, as a combination of crustal down-warping and flooding, which buried organic sediment deep beneath the region. It takes time, but continental plates do slowly shift, changing the face of the world. Experts have concluded that the Barnett Shale deposit may have the largest producible reserves from an onshore natural gas field in this country. While many residents have welcomed the infusion of wealth associated with gas production, there have also been concerns of environmental and aesthetic considerations because so much of the gas-rich shale lies underneath heavily urbanized areas like Arlington and Fort Worth. Though the gas production of such wells tends, on average, to diminish sharply in very few years, the current extraction techniques tend to capture only a small portion of the gas trapped in the shale. The expectation is that as extraction technology improves, drilling and extraction will continue, presumably and hopefully with less impact on the urban environment.

The presence of the Barnett Shale demonstrates, however, that the past absolutely impacts the present and the future. Where you are and what happened long ago—even more than 300 million years ago—matters.

That the "where" of a place matters was often pointed out succinctly with reliable consistency by Arlington's legendary former mayor, Tom Vandergriff. Arlington's top asset has always been, he said, "Location, location and location." Vandergriff was talking about geographic location, but he might as well have included geology in the process.

Urban sociologist Max Weber said that cities, even those functioning at the most basic level, have to do at least two things: offer a minimally hospitable environment and provide adequate access to food, water and building materials. But to actually prosper, Weber said, cities must do even more. They may be situated at a natural crossroad, offer a break point for transportation purposes, access raw materials like cotton or iron ore, provide some special amenity like a beach or skiing, serve administrative, military or political purpose, or function as a religious or educational center.

In differing degrees and at various times, Arlington has somehow found a way, by luck, leadership, purpose or design of the Great Master Planner, to perform all of Weber's points of prosperity, aided greatly through an almost-accident of location.

Contemplate that "minimally hospitable environment" consideration. With an annual rainfall of 32 inches, Arlington splits sub-arid and humid zones and sits on a juncture of life forms in a north-south, temperate-to-subtropical distribution. The city is also divided into two geological strata—woodlands and prairie. Although the terrain by comparison to some other parts of the world is not particularly picturesque in the way that mountain vistas or ocean beaches provide appeal, there's usually plenty of water, occasional droughts not-withstanding. It's rarely extremely cold for long, that particular condition depending almost entirely on the arrival of "blue northers" that originate in Canada or the north Pacific. When the northers fade away, warm Gulf of Mexico breezes quickly work their way northward. It can and does snow in North Texas, but it is not uncommon for entire winters to pass without a single snowflake sticking to the sprawling city's suburban lawns.

It is not snow sled country. Summers can be brutal. Drought is not uncommon. The summer of 2011, for instance, had more than 71 days when the temperature hit 100 degrees or more. In many ways the Eastern Cross Timbers is a kind of transitional geography marking the turning point between eastern Texas with its abundant rainfall and an increasingly arid west, where annual precipitation drops an inch for each county stretching westward. Perhaps this explains why early settlers to Arlington were mostly farmers, even as neighboring Fort Worth became famous as "Cowtown."

Those resources, a bountiful mix of woodlands and prairie, were important to humankind's existence in the Arlington area long before the first Anglo settlers put down tent stakes and began building log cabins.

The year before Lake Arlington filled in April of 1957, an archaeological dig was conducted along Arlington's Village Creek. That dig turned up evidence of pre-Indian humans living along the Trinity River tributary at least 7,000 years ago. But people have lived here much longer than that, recent discoveries pointing to humans living here and elsewhere in Texas as much as 15,000 years ago. Indeed, if the trend continues, future discoveries will find evidence of human habitation even further back.

Then again, historically and geologically speaking, 7,000 years ranks as a mere speck in time. As noted earlier in this chapter, there was a period when at least half of Arlington really did have a beach, though that's been a while, harking back to the Cretaceous era of about 95 million years ago when Arlington was the beachhead for a warm and giant shallow sea that almost divided the continent. With an ebb here and a flow there, the former sea is now part of eastern Arlington and called the Eagle Ford. Once that salty plain received a few million years of rainfall it became a prairie, the legendary "Sea of Grass." The hilly western part of the city, once an alluvial beach (that's geology talk for a place where fresh water flows dump sandy sediment) is usually referred to as the Eastern Cross Timbers, though the region's east is Arlington's west. The city's rolling west-side hills, now laden with oaks are, in fact, ancient sand dunes, churned up by a mixture of oceanic waves pounding the shores even as ancient rivers and creeks carried sand and sediment to the sea.

Historical geographer Richard Francaviglia, author of "The Cast Iron Forest," may well be the world's leading authority on the Cross Timber woodlands that distinguish western Arlington from its eastern prairie. He notes that though urban landscapes have tamed the forest oak population, it was once quite dense, so much so that it was virtually impossible to drive a wagon through it.

"Home to Native Americans over several thousand years, the Cross Timbers were considered a barrier to westward expansion in the nineteenth century, until roads and railroads opened up the region to farmers, ranchers, coal miners and modern city developers, all of whom changed its character in far-reaching ways," Francaviglia said. "The presence of these forests amidst prairie both interested and perplexed early travelers. To some, the Cross Timbers appeared to be a huge island, or perhaps a peninsula, of dense forest rising from a sea of grass."

None other than Washington Irving, a man of letters famed for creation of characters like Ichabod Crane, took note of the Cross Timbers when he traveled through the region in 1832. There's this comment from his "A Tour of the Prairie."

"I shall not easily forget the mortal toil, and the vexations of flesh and spirit, that we underwent occasionally, in our wanderings through the Cross Timber," Irving wrote. "It was like struggling through forests of cast iron."

Arlington's location as a city where prairie and woodlands meet (some have said it was where the Old South ended and the West began) also was an important factor to both early Native Americans and Anglo pioneers from a land navigation perspective. Anyone with a rough and rudimentary idea of the geography of the region could find the Arlington area easily enough, either by following the melding edge of the woodlands (Woodbine aka Eastern Cross Timbers) and prairie (the Eagle Ford aka Grand Prairie) to the Trinity, or by finding the Trinity itself and following it to that point where oak forest became head-high grassland. It's another one of those coincidental "location, location, location" things. But it was not a coincidence, for example, that the first attempted Anglo settlement area was at just that juncture in what is now far North Arlington, but which was then called Bird's Fort, a three-minute stroll from the aforementioned Arlington Archosaur Site.

But leaving that kind of history to the paleontologists and archeologists, most of the interest in the history of the area focuses on more recent developments of the past few hundred years.

In North Texas for hundreds of years before Anglo/Europeans arrived, the prevailing dominant culture in North Texas was the Caddo Indians, "Caddo" being a mispronunciation of Kodohadach. Caddos have several tribes but scholars generally agree that the linguistic family includes the Wichita, Kichai, Pawnee and Arikara tribes.

Caddos, who also appear to have Mayan roots or at least some of their characteristics, represent the zenith of Indian cultural and social development in Texas. From 1536, when Cabeza DeVaca and other Spanish and French explorers began penetrating the region, they discovered Caddos operating trade routes over land and waterways, growing crops that varied from corn and squash to sunflower seeds, and even indulging in quasi-commercial fishing with a multi-hooked Caddo invention that Texans know more familiarly as a trotline. Archeologists believe that the Caddos or their ancestors were in this region a thousand years before the first Europeans showed up.

In short, the Caddos—of which perhaps only 500 with relatively pure bloodlines are left today—were attracted to this area because it was a location to their liking with many waterways, a buffalo-filled prairie, game-filled woodlands and a climate that was reasonably hospitable to agriculture. It also was a site that would be coveted by many others, much to the agitation of the dominant Caddo branch in the Arlington area, the Hasinai. Scholars disagree on how many tribal branches of Caddos existed, perhaps as many as 23, but the divisions were themselves so frequently competitive that by the 1800s the Caddos were in no position to resist encroachment by others.

"When Europeans first arrived, the Caddo were settled, farming people who grew corn, beans, squash, sunflowers, and other crops and lived in farmsteads, hamlets, and villages strung out along streams and rivers that mainly flow to the east and south through their homeland," wrote Susan Dial, the co-editor of "Texas Beyond History."

The Caddo decline probably began with their first exposure to European diseases such as measles and smallpox, to which they had no resistance. By 1800 their numbers had been so decimated that their territories were steadily being taken, first by other Indian tribes and then pioneer settlers. That Caddo decline—a better word would be "displacement"—was accelerated by settlement in Southeast Texas by

Moses and Stephen Austin beginning in 1821 and by the Federal Indian Relocation Act of 1830, which resulted in many tribes fleeing westward to Texas, not then part of the United States. By 1835, more than a dozen tribes ranging from nomadic Kiowas and Comanches to Cherokees and tribal remnants from other states had moved into what is now the Metroplex area.

It was a classic frontier situation and one in which conflict with ever-expanding Anglo settlements was inevitable. The Indians were fleeing what amounted to U.S. aggression and land grabs. When Texas settlers waged war against Mexico for the independence that came in 1836, Indians in the future Metroplex area were initially left to their own devices. That changed quickly after the Texas Revolutionary War. In the early days of the Republic, the Indians tended to be the superior fighters, both individually and militarily. For example in the 1830s a group of Anglo hunters were attacked and scalped near the site of Arlington's present-day landfill near the Trinity River. In 1838 a Texan military foray from Fannin County, commanded by Robert Sloan and Nathanial Journey (the Sloan-Journey Expedition), set up an ambush in the same area, killing all the members of a Caddo hunting party.

Smaller skirmishes were common. Though populations varied, the Village and Rush Creek areas in present-day west Arlington were estimated by early Euro-settlers to host as many as 25,000 Indians. This speculation, if accurate, would have given what would become Arlington one of the most concentrated populations of Native Americans on the North American continent. If so, it was quite likely an untypical condition greatly related to displacement of Indian populations in the U.S. It also was likely the maximum population that the area could support even under ideal environmental conditions.

A series of archaeological digs on a section of Village Creek south of Lake Arlington, conducted from 1994 – 1996 by University of Texas at Arlington students under the direction of Anthropology Professor Jeffery Hanson, found evidence of extensive early occupation and an agricultural society.

Finds included stone tools and flint flakings—flint does not naturally occur in the area—an assortment of more than 40 varied projectile points, bone tools, a storage hole, and signs of semi-permanent habitation and pottery shards. Hanson considers the shards particularly significant because they tend to indicate permanent residency. "Nomads don't use pottery," Hanson said. "It's too fragile."

Dating techniques put the age of the students' finds anywhere from 1,500 B.C. to 1,500 A.D. Later digs near the Trinity River, in what is now River Legacy Parks, added further confirmation to the presence of significant quantities of Native Americans for centuries before Europeans or their descendants arrived.

Despite the dangers, attempts by Anglos to settle the area were inevitable. The first such endeavor involving newly-arriving Texans came with an 1841 expedition led by Major Jonathan Bird to establish a fort on a small oxbow pond adjoining the Trinity River a couple of miles east of modern-day Collins Street (a historical marker nearby incorrectly notes the year as 1840).

Why this particular location? Most likely it was because from a navigational purpose it was easy enough to locate. As noted earlier in this chapter, the trick was to either find the Trinity and follow it along the prairie until it intersected the wooded Eastern Cross Timbers, or find the Eastern Cross Timbers first and follow the eastern edge until the Trinity emerges. By pioneer standards this was an easy location to find, possible even if—for example—a navigation error of 50 miles or so was made. Never mind that the spot was difficult to defend militarily and was subject to frequent flooding! In one of those quirks of urban development or non-development, the Bird's Fort area remained undeveloped for most of Arlington's history, only recently becoming the focus of residential and commercial efforts.

Area Indians were familiar with Major Bird, though not in a positive way. Bird, an experienced scout and Indian fighter, had earlier led an attack on an Indian camp on Village Creek near its intersection with the Trinity River. Still seething with understandable rage and a need

35

for revenge, area Indians burned off adjoining areas around the fort to eliminate stock grazing and easy hunting. They also picked off stragglers and made the area so dangerous that Bird was forced to twice-abandon the fort in favor of a new village a few miles east—a place that would be called Dallas. Bird's Fort is long gone but the pond adjoining the makeshift fortification is still around, the pond commonly called Callaway Lake.

As for Bird—as admired by newly arriving pioneers as he was disliked by Indians—a new town called Birdville was eventually named after him. Today it's called Haltom City, though the school district that serves that city and several others is still called the Birdville Independent School District. Bird's Fort quickly disappeared, becoming little more than a footnote in Arlington's history, albeit with a couple of provisos. Later on it would be the site of an Indian raid on a federal gold shipment, and also would serve as a meeting place for the ill-fated Santa Fe expedition.

The "Indian problem" as characterized by the demise of Bird's Fort so antagonized the rabidly anti-Indian Gen. E.H. Tarrant (Yes, Tarrant County's namesake, though he was at the time but a captain), that he mounted a punitive expedition in 1841 that culminated in what historians billed as the Battle of Village Creek. Though the historical marker that outlines the details of the battle is located on Pioneer Parkway Boulevard in Arlington just north of Lake Arlington, most historians think the encounter took place along Village Creek a few miles further north toward the Trinity near the juncture of Rush and Village creeks, or very close to today's Division Street. Tarrant's 69-man militia was lucky to arrive at the creek area of what's now west Arlington when most of the warriors were away on a buffalo hunt. Tarrant's expedition found several villages—some occupied and some not—and also an estimated 300 acres of corn under cultivation.

The attack resulted in an estimated dozen or so Indian casualties and the death of Denton County namesake John Denton, ambushed as he recklessly attempted to pursue retreating Indians across a brushy area. A

Frontier Times article published in 1931 noted that Denton, a Methodist preacher and an attorney, was unlucky enough to pursue not the expected Caddos, but considerably more deadly Comanches, resulting in his death and the wounding of at least two other pursuers.

His body was buried near a creek near Denton County, the grave concealed so as to prevent Indian discovery, concealed so well that his relatives searching for it in 1849 could not find it. Were it not for the discovery of a body in a shallow grave by cowboys working for the legendary John Chisum in 1861, Denton's body might never have been found. Identified through some gold fillings, a personal tin cup and evidence of a previously broken arm, Denton's body's was moved to a grave at Chisum's ranch, only later to be reburied with considerable ceremony in Denton County in 1901.

After the battle, Major Bird attempted to resettle his fort, but with results identical to his first effort. The Indian problem persisted. The fort was abandoned again in 1842 and the area for more than a century and a half was mostly used for landfills, gravel mining and horse riding. In the interim, little Arlington grew from a half-square-mile village to almost 100 square miles.

By 1843, Texas President Sam Houston, historically considered more conciliatory and sympathetic to Indians than his Texas countrymen, decided that a preferable solution was to work out a peaceful solution with the Indians of the region, in short a treaty. The proposed "Treaty of Bird's Fort" would establish a series of trading and military posts to separate the factions. Houston himself came to then unnamed Arlington to negotiate the treaty, most likely camping at Marrow Bone Springs in what is now Pioneer Park immediately southeast of the intersection of modern-day Arkansas Lane and Matlock Road. A spring that is still flowing there was a common camp site for both Indians returning from buffalo hunts, and for Anglo adventurers looking for a campsite with water.

The "Marrow Bone" name probably came from the presence of thousands of bison bones roasted for their marrow. An archeological "dig" around the spring would no doubt provide more than a few historical treasures and insights.

The chiefs of the Indian tribes were slow to arrive and Houston was forced to depart before their arrival, but he left his representatives to work out details of a "Treaty of Peace and Friendship." This Treaty also known as the Treaty of Bird's Fort, was to establish a trading post in yet-unnamed Arlington and leave the Indians territory north of the Trinity River.

The agreement, the first treaty that the Republic of Texas would sign with any Indian tribes, gave the Indians an assortment of goods valued at an estimated $89, essentially opening up for settlement the area from Waco north to what would become the Metroplex. The new Republic of Texas also made good on its promise to open a trading post at which Indians could swaps goods. The post eventually ended up being run by war hero Col. Middleton Tate Johnson. Johnson Station being the first settlement with any staying power, in what would later become Arlington. The station on Mayfield Road (originally Johnson-Mask Road) was located about a mile southwest of Marrow Bone Springs. A small historical marker is the only hint of the trading station's former existence.

By the time of the treaty offer the various tribes that had moved into the area to escape U.S. expansion were weary of running and were ready for a peace settlement.

The question: Why would the Indians, with obvious numerical and military superiority, agree to such terms? Many historians have debated the topic, but it seems clear that many of the tribes were themselves new to the region and felt no particular sense of ownership. Too, the various tribes of that era were sometimes more competitive than cooperative. They also were weary after literally being chased westward for more than a decade. Nor did they perhaps realize that the hastily formed and quickly disbanded Texan militias of the time—though composed of hardened men—were in no way as relentless or as efficient as the disciplined, trained and well-equipped U.S. Cavalry.

The treaty pow-wow at Marrow Bone Springs made this desire for peace by many tribal chiefs, like Delaware Chief Roasting Ear, evident.

"I am anxious that all things between the white man and the red man should go on right," Roasting Ear said during the meeting. "For this reason, Delawares and Chickasaws here came so far from their homes and are here to bring about a good understanding between them. Listen to me. We are like the children of one mother, the same people. We are all the same color, all red men. I want you to continue to walk in the white path and be like the red men of the old nations in the United States. They hear the talk of the white man and they keep his counsel. For that reason there is no trouble amongst them. I want the red men of this country to do the same thing."

It should be noted that the more militant and aggressive Indian tribes—specifically the Kiowas, Comanches and Apaches—did not sign the Treaty of Bird's Fort. Although historians list the Battle of Village Creek (some call this the "Keechi Village Fight") as the final Indian battle in what would become Tarrant County, skirmishes continued, including an unsuccessful 1858 attack by an estimated 200 Comanches on nearby Johnson Station. This attack, and a separate incident involving the slaughter of a family that is buried in the Tomlin Cemetery, prompted the U.S. Army to step up its activity in the region after Texas joined the union. One of the officers to command troops in the area was a recent West Point graduate who would eventually become one of the Army's most gifted tacticians, a young lieutenant named Robert E. Lee.

As for the Indians in the area, a proviso of Texas' inclusion as the 28th state on Dec. 29, 1845, was that all previous treaties signed by the Texas Republic were voided. Whatever deals the Republic of Texas had made with Indian tribes were cancelled, certainly not the first or last double cross Native Americans would endure. The Indians in the area were first relocated to a reservation on the Brazos River in Young County near Graham a hundred miles west, and eventually from there to Oklahoma in the 1860s.

With the Indian "problem" more or less resolved, many settlers began moving into the area. One of the advantages of the "Sea of Grass," the prairie, was that it could be easily plowed. And the dense post oak and blackjack woodlands made for easily accessible home and building materials. Johnson Station would begin to grow and prosper, though most of its residents would eventually decide to move a few miles due north when the Texas and Pacific Railroad showed up. This new place would be called Arlington.

Chapter 3 – Frontier Days

American frontiersman and Alamo hero Davy Crockett shared a sentiment with many pioneers who ventured to Arlington in the mid-1800s: Anytime the smoke of a neighbor's chimney could be seen, it meant civilization was about to arrive. To Crockett's restless mind this meant the neighborhood was getting too crowded and it was time to move on. For many such adventurers, Arlington—then better known as Johnson Station—was the jumping off point to the West. Or, the place to set up a homestead because Indian problems made it too dangerous to venture further.

Bird's Fort, an 1841 attempt by Maj. Jonathan Bird to establish a foothold in the area, failed. But the trading post that Republic of Texas President Sam Houston had promised Native Americans in the 1844 Treaty of Bird's Fort was originally established by Indian trader Mathias Travis as Texas Trading Post No. 1. It is located on what is now Mayfield Road between Cooper Street and Matlock Road, a site now identifiable only by a small historical marker. The trading post was next to a small creek, now called Johnson Creek, that flows northeasterly through nearby Marrow Bone Springs on its way to the Trinity River. It was the Marrow Bones Springs site that most historians think actually hosted the treaty parley with a dozen Indian tribes that led to creation of the trading post, though two historical markers in Arlington claim this distinction.

The trading post quickly became the headquarters for a Texas Rangers' company commanded by Col. Middleton Tate Johnson, a veteran of the war with Mexico and a personal friend and admirer of Houston.

Like many early Americans, Johnson had always had an itch to move west. Born in South Carolina, he moved to Georgia as a boy and came to Texas by way of Alabama, where he served four terms in the state legislature before moving—for reasons that remain unclear—to Shelby County, Texas, in 1839. Shelby County turned out to be a place in ferment. Frictions between a vigilante faction and an anti-vigilante group—the Regulators and the Moderators—turned into a feud over land titles and other disagreements that left the landscape riddled with casualties, some shot, some stabbed and some hung, both sides claiming to have the law on their side. Houston was so irritated by the conflict that he threatened removal of the county from Texas.

Johnson was a captain for the Regulators, though not the commanding officer, but was nevertheless of high enough stature to make him the designated recipient of a disbandment agreement.

Both the Regulators and Moderators honored the disbandment and abandoned the feud to partake in the Mexican War, at the conclusion of which Johnson—by then a colonel—evidently decided that the better part of prudence would be to move out of Shelby County. Houston appointed him as a Texas Rangers commander. Johnson liked what he found in the future Arlington so much that when Texas joined the United States (Dec. 29, 1845) and his military duties ended, he bought land. He also bought the trading post. Fancying himself as an Old South plantation owner, he purchased slaves—as many as 80—and began Southern-style cotton farming. Arlington's early reliance on slave labor is an often-overlooked component of the city's history. The plantation would have been located between present-day Cooper and Center streets and south of Arkansas Lane, including what is now The Parks of Arlington Mall.

Though Indian attacks diminished after Texas became a state, Arlington was not yet secure. Skirmishes continued, including an unsuccessful 1858 attack on Johnson Station by an estimated 200 Comanches. This attack and separate incidents involving the murder, allegedly by Comanches, of a Caddo Indian named Pantego—namesake for that small community—and the slaughter of a local family in north Arlington (now buried in the Tomlin Family Cemetery), prompted the U.S. Army to step up its activities in the region. Many of those federal officers given duty in North Texas would later become prominent in the Civil War, the most notable being a young West Point lieutenant named Robert E. Lee.

What about the provisions of the Treaty of Bird's Fort between the Republic of Texas and the area's Indian tribes? One of the requirements of Texas becoming the 28th state was that all previous treaties signed by the nation of Texas, with Indians or other nations, were void. Indians in the area—those that cooperated, at least—were first relocated to Young County near Graham about 100 miles west, and eventually from there to Oklahoma during the 1860s.

Johnson Station was on stage and wagon train routes, with the station and plantation quickly evolving into a growing operation abated only slightly by the Civil War (1861-65). As a kind of jumping-off place to the frontier, the station quickly filled up with out-of-work soldiers and rangers, adventurers, sodbusters, buffalo hunters, merchants, gamblers, land speculators and the assorted desperados who always seem to live on the edge of frontiers. It was a risky sort of existence, full of people who endorsed another of Davy Crockett's famous ideas: *Everybody out East could go to Hell. They were going to Texas.*

Early Stagecoach

Settlers, would-be farmers in particular, liked the idea of a prairie place where a plow could mark its furrows without the constant back-breaking clearing of stumps and rocks, though no doubt that first plow mark through grass-laced sod would be difficult enough. In particular the pastoral beauty of the prairie in spring often was, historian Arista Joyner said, "a wonderment to travelers."

"In some parts of the prairie the grasses grew so high the horses had to breast their way through it," she wrote. "But, in other places, the whole prairie was covered with all colors and kinds of flowering growth. One child gathered as many as forty different kinds of flowers on one of the short coach stops. A favorite sky-colored flower of the travelers was one that grew on a stalk, each of its flowers looking like a sweet pea. It was called the bluebonnet—the future state flower of Texas."

Once tamed, the prairie could yield much more than grass and flowers. It could deliver wheat and corn, beans, melons, potatoes and sorghum. And, of course, the Southern king of cash crops: cotton.

Cities are sometimes created—or not—on whims or notions. Thus it was that Johnson was visited in 1853 by Army Captain Ripley Arnold, who had been advised by Houston to seek the colonel's counsel on the best location for a new fort. Arnold and his dragoons (dragoons are essentially mounted infantry) had been operating out of Fort Graham near Hillsboro (the fort is now beneath the waters of Lake Whitney) but the Army needed a more strategic location further north. Historians can only guess at Johnson's motives, but instead of a location near his plantation he suggested a site a few miles west of Johnson Station near the confluence of the West and Clear forks of the Trinity.

Had Johnson selected a fort location a bit closer to the plantation, the decision would likely have resulted in there being no future Arlington at all. Johnson and Arnold decided to name the new fort after their commander in the Mexican War, Major General William Worth. A thriving community would boom around the fort. It would be called Fort Worth. Johnson, who conveniently owned land near the fort, donated the site for the new city's first courthouse. Johnson would eventually become known as the father of Tarrant County, though in one of those odd quirks of happenstance, it would be Johnson County that would be named after him.

After failing in the last of several tries for the Texas governorship, Johnson—by then a ceaseless advocate for a railroad that would provide easy access to his plantation products—became ill shortly after being elected to the state's reconstruction convention in 1865. He died in 1866 as he was returning from south Texas. His death really marked the end of the pioneering era and the beginning of the settlement phase. Though clearly an enigma—a blend of politician, Indian fighter, merchant, soldier, Civil War gun runner, Rhett Butler-style blockade buster and slave owner—Johnson was not only the most dominant and important personality in Arlington's pioneer history but also for all of Tarrant County. Johnson is buried today in the Johnson Plantation Cemetery on Arkansas Lane about a hundred yards west of Matlock Road. Other Johnson family members lie at rest on the east side of the cemetery, with slaves and their descendants on the west.

If Johnson was the most important figure in Arlington's pioneer history, the runner-up would have to be a visionary Cumberland Presbyterian minister, Andrew Hayter (pronounced Hi-Der), who had established a small congregation near Johnson Station in 1853. When it was announced that the long-awaited Texas and Pacific Railroad line would pass through three miles north, Hayter decided that the future of the community was there. He recommended a new settlement near the future railroad and much of his flock agreed to make the move. One of the consistencies in American pioneer communities is that popular ministers tended to provide leadership in many more areas than just the spiritual realm.

Like most country ministers of his day, Hayter couldn't make a living as a preacher alone. He was the proverbial jack of all trades. He was an expert surveyor, knew how to mill lumber from the region's tough little oaks and regularly made Bowie-like knives, which meant he also had blacksmithing skills. The little community he founded no longer exists but was originally located near present-day Texas 360 and Interstate 20, the rough hamlet named by community members as West Fork. The Watson Cemetery is all that remains of West Fork.

The Texas and Pacific Railroad wanting a fuel and loading stop midway between Dallas and Fort Worth, hired Hayter to both survey the future small community and to contract for railroad ties. Though he probably knew the decision would ultimately mean both the end of West Fork and Johnson Station, Hayter picked the present-day route as the most viable, a more northerly route through West Fork having the disadvantage of having to cross an oft-flooded lowlands near the merger of Rush and Village creeks.

Thousands of communities across this country got their start the same way that Arlington began: They began as empty acreage on a railroad route. The object of those who build railroads is to make money, initially by selling tracts of land to make new communities, which then themselves need the rails to ship their cattle, cotton and coal and receive their new fabrics, tools and foodstuffs, creating an economic synergy of incredible potency.

The community that Hayter and the railroad surveyed was a half-mile by half-mile, divided into 100-yard blocks, the center of which was—imagination was not a priority in such situations—Center and Main streets. The edges of the new, as-yet-unnamed place, were simple as well. North and south boundaries (but running east and west) were North and South streets. East and west boundaries (but running north and south) were East and West streets.

As for the train, the Texas and Pacific Engine No. 20 rolled through in 1878. If the definition of having arrived in frontier Texas could be defined as the ability to buy a railroad ticket to go there, the question was this: A train ticket to where? What would be the name of this place?

The railroad appreciated Hayter's services and apparently gave him naming privileges, though by then old and new arrivals alike were already calling it Hayterville, as often as not mispronouncing it as Hate-Ur-Ville, a name with a decidedly unpleasant ring. Hayter and this new place's second postmaster, Jim Ditto, originally proposed that the new city be labeled Johnson City in honor of Col. Johnson, but the post office turned down that name on the grounds that it was too close to Johnson Station.

First Downtown Arlington

Hayter and Ditto then made a peculiar decision. Both had met Robert E. Lee when he served in North Texas as an Indian fighter commanding the Dragoons. As Southern sympathizers their respect had not diminished when Lee became commanding general of the Confederacy. Ditto and Hayter proposed that the city be the first and only Arlington in Texas—Arlington also being both the name of Lee's hometown in Virginia and of his residence there, Arlington House. The postmaster general—no doubt not making the connection—approved the name in 1865. Hayter did not die until 1900, an occasion for which the town wept, as towns tend to do when a local legend finally passes away.

But a survey by itself does not a community make, even if there is an official post office designation. Initially, there was no formal governance. Functioning informally, law enforcement was handled through a sort of general community appointment of a Judge Roy Bean-style moderator named John Huitt, whose punishments were often deemed too draconian by even frontier standards. Huitt was followed by creation of a Shelby County-style group of vigilantes who called themselves Liberators, who themselves were countered by yet another group who dubbed themselves Moderators. Neither group—both considerably less violent than their counterparts in Shelby County—produced satisfactory outcomes to everyone concerned.

When that first train pulled into town in 1876 there was not yet much town to see. According to an account in the Arlington Citizen by long-time resident and editor S.R. Perry, there were, in fact, only two stores and four houses. The stores included two general purpose stores, one owned by Jim Ditto and another by Preston Rose, Ditto and Rose both being names that would be prominent in the city's future.

But a small hotel and boarding house quickly showed up. George Lampe built a blacksmith shop, and a fellow recalled by history only as "Rector" built a livery stable, all constructed along dirt streets. But more people kept arriving; the population growing to about 200 by incorporation in 1884—500 if those living just outside city limits were counted.

Arlington would have many identities in the years to come, but in 1884 the big industry was cotton ginning. Arlington was a place for farmers in the region to bring short and medium staple cotton, botanically termed Gossypium Hirsutum, for processing and bailing, selling it to buyers, who in turn hauled it to the Main Street station and packed it aboard trains headed for big cloth mills back east and even Europe. By 1890, Arlington had five such cotton gins.

Perhaps the village had one or two more saloons than gins. Farmers and farmhands often spent their hard-earned dollars at the general store, perhaps stopping for a beer and free sandwich at one of the saloons. It was trickle-down agrarian economics at work, extremely simplistic but reasonably efficient, so much so that the town kept growing. It had a doctor and even its first newspaper in 1883, The World, which would ultimately evolve into the Arlington Democrat and from there to the Arlington Journal, the Arlington Citizen-Journal and finally to the Arlington Star-Telegram.

Farm hands were mostly black laborers who had gone from working for nothing as slaves to being paid very little for their toil as free people. The farmers, of course, didn't see it that way. In the Arlington Democrat, farmer J.W. Doherty complained that he had to pay 50 cents a day for good hired help, the "work day" essentially being sunup to sundown, lunch included. But then again, a dollar in this era stretched considerably further than in more recent times. The average home sold for about $500.

Early Arlington Church

Churches

Because religion was so important spiritually, socially and politically, churches started popping up before Arlington even had official status.

Methodist Church

Though Presbyterians founded the town, the first church within city limits was First United Methodist Church, which began meeting in 1877 at Shultz's Lumber Yard.

Baptist Church

First Baptist Church, which came into being a year earlier at Johnson Station, eventually moved to the new town as well—both churches growing and remaining in the heart of the original community to this day.

And there were others to come, such as Rehoboth Baptist in south Arlington, dating from 1870. And Tate Springs Baptist, 1882; New Hope Baptist, 1885; First Presbyterian and Mission Ridge Cumberland Presbyterian, both 1888; and First Christian Church, 1893. Woods Chapel Baptist came along in 1901. Arlington today has more than a dozen prospering churches with history dating back more than a century.

An early newspaper editor looked at the proliferation of churches—the city had not quite 1,000 residents by 1900—and remarked that the Baptists seemed "to be running everything, but that when you come down to it, the Methodists own everything."

This was a logical observation. Original townspeople, the majority of whom were property and store owners, tended to join the first formal protestant church to show up, that being the Methodists. A community can only grow so much, of course, before it requires services, regulations and the laws that bring with them a sense of security and predictability. It was apparent that to be a city run by law and with protections of law, formal status as a city was necessary.

Becoming a city was not a particularly complex arrangement. Community leaders wrote a dozen proposed ordinances, and then they filed for official municipal incorporation at the county courthouse, formally and officially becoming Arlington, Texas, on April 21, 1884. Townspeople elected George Finger as the city's first mayor and the council named A.J. Rogers as the Town Council secretary. The ordinances reflected the community's chief concerns, probably in order of those concerns. Here's the wording of Ordinance No. 1, which was aimed at preventing the carrying of weapons:

1. *Be it ordained by the Town Council of the Town of Arlington: That any person who shall, within the limits of the Town of Arlington, carry on or about his person, saddle or in his saddle bags, any pistol, dirk, dagger, sling shot, sword cane, spear, brass knuckles, bowie-knife, or any other kind of knife manufactured or sold for purposes of offense or defense, shall be deemed guilty of a misdemeanor and upon conviction shall be fined not less than twenty-five nor more than one hundred dollars.*

Clearly the city's newly anointed founding fathers wanted to put a stop to the gun-toting, knife-carrying tendencies of the populace. The other eleven ordinances in summary were:

2. *Prohibiting the indecent exposure of person (quite likely a reaction to the bawdy bar and prostitute scene that was part of nearby Fort Worth Hell's Acre district).*

3. *Governing sale of liquors.*

4. *Prohibiting riding of horses or other livestock into houses (evidently a big enough problem to warrant an ordinance).*

5. *A Sunday blue law prohibiting commerce on the Sabbath (keep in mind that Arlington was essentially started by hard core Presbyterians in search of a railroad).*

6. *Business and meetings in Council (where and when)*

7. *Concerning carcasses of dead animals (Some people tended to be a bit sloppy about disposal of unwanted body parts after slaughter).*

8. *Prohibiting offenses against the peace.*

9. *Powers and duties of aldermen.*

10. *Regulating stoppage of animals and vehicles.*

11. *Vagrancy (the aldermen wanted no part of the idle hang-around crowd that characterized Johnson Station)*

12. *Prohibited gaming.*

Quite clearly the newly-created Arlington community and its leaders wanted an orderly sort of place. Their first ordinances focused on stopping violence or unruly behavior, controlling liquor, gambling and prostitution, respecting religion and eliminating the town as a kind of stopover for adventurers, cowboys or soldiers between jobs. In short, not to be another Fort Worth, or a Fort Worth as it was then. In such agrarian communities the mayor often serves as chief magistrate and municipal employees are few in number, perhaps none at all or limited to a part-time town marshal. If there was a major deficiency in Arlington's initial dozen ordinances it was that there was no provision for the town to somehow collect revenues. But that oversight would be rectified soon enough. Every government gets around to taxes sooner than later.

The story of the town's creation was celebrated in some detail by the town newspaper, The World. The paper had been established a year earlier, 1883, by lumber yard operator Col. Thomas Spruance and Willis Timmerman. Timmerman, the paper's editor and later the town mayor, printed it one page at a time on an old Washington-style sheet press kept in a shed near the Main Street train station. Timmerman was a natural gossip, collecting bits and pieces from train travelers as well as gathering information from magazines and newspapers the travelers brought with them.

If the incorporation of Arlington as an official community was The World's first big story, the next big one would come on March 15, 1885, when the city's cash flow source, the railroad line, hit a major snag when Texas and Pacific Railroad's Engine No 643 went off the tracks at the Village Creek Bridge. The crash killed the train's fireman and injured several others.

"Torrential rains have been falling over most of Central Texas and Louisiana and flooded conditions here caused the trestle at Village Creek to give way," Timmerman wrote in The World. "The engine, pulling passenger train No 304, was headed east down the long hill from Handley. The water at that time was twelve feet deep and the trestle was about sixteen feet above the water. It began to give way when the front wheels struck the bridge, and although the train was moving at only twelve miles an hour, the momentum caused the mail car to fall on the engine and it in turn was pushed downstream by the baggage car. The Pacific Company was believed to have lost some money packages. Among the passengers was an aggregation of the Peck's Bad Boy group."

Peck's Bad Boys? This was a theatrical group based on popular characters featuring a mischievous boy created by writer George W. Peck. The wreck caused the group's members to miss their next performance in Dallas.

Residents flocked to the bridge to try to pull the engine out, but rains continued and the engine sank steadily into the quicksand, eventually the engine being deemed a total loss. It remains there today beneath the surface, an iron horse mixed with concrete from generations of new bridge pilings. The loss of the engine combined with the expense of maintaining the line might well have been a fatal blow for the train company, which soon thereafter was forced to file for bankruptcy.

Such setbacks aside, Mayor Finger—as mayors everywhere tend to do—predicted a great future for the little dusty-street town of a few hundred people, located as it was, he said, "Right square dab in the middle" between Dallas and Fort Worth. Finger's version of the "location, location" refrain was probably the first such politically-tinged refrain in the city's history. But it certainly wouldn't be the last.

Arlington's central location and access to the train quickly made the town a kind of agrarian trade center. Although cotton continued as the mainstream business, on Saturday the town's population would swell by the hundreds when people came to town, as Arista Joyner noted, to trade for horses or mules, to buy or sell hay, oats, peanuts, sweet and Irish potatoes, sorghum, peas and other vegetables, and to compete for prizes for growing the biggest watermelon or pumpkin. Or perhaps to swap a yearling pig for other provisions.

But the surge in popularity—particularly the weekend crowd—produced a thirsty problem. The small, shallow wells that homeowners and businesses dug were simply insufficient for public purposes. Indeed, the weekend market crowd alone was sufficient to completely empty some of the small wells. Visitors and their horses needed a steady supply of water. Local businessman Rice Woods Collins (his family is the namesake for Collins Street) began a two-year collection campaign to fund the building of such a well. The decision was to put it in the middle of the intersection of Center and Main streets. In Joyner's view it turned out to be one of the worst decisions in the city's history.

"Much to the disgust and surprise of the residents, the water turned out to be mineral water!" Joyner wrote. "It smelled bad and tasted bad also. It was dubbed 'Carlsbad' water."

Original Mineral Water Well

Worse, once tapped, the water streamed to the surface with a steady flow as if the earth was expelling it, the stinky water running steadily down Center Street, initially at an estimated quagmirish 50,000 gallons a day. The city built a large wooden trough—the first of many well embellishments—for horses, most of which declined to drink it, as did everything and everyone else.

Collins made the most of it, claiming that the water had medical properties that would be a boon to the health of local residents and an attraction to commerce. Though clearly unhappy at the turn of events, merchants adopted a wait-and-see attitude. A few even began advertising mineral baths.

The city tried to make the most of the well, sprinkling it to dry on dusty streets, where it left a ghostly white residue that—in time—coated just about everything with a white pallor. Would-be entrepreneurs would eventually tap their own wells into the water strata—the same strata that gave the name "Mineral Wells" to another Texas city—and to boil it into Epson salts-like crystals dubbed "Arlington crystals," a business that lasted until the 1950s.

Innovation seems to work best when it replaces drudgery. And no doubt Arlington's hard-working residents were weary of humdrum tasks. For the women, cooking, ironing, churning, baking, sewing and mending grew tiresome. The same could be said for the men with their plowing, planting, hoeing, repairing, harvesting, taking care of stock and bartering. They craved ways to make life a little less difficult—a little more comfortable.

Arlington's water system, for example, had its origins in the unglamorous calling of J.W. Hammack's pig farm operation. After complaining of "wearing out my arms" carrying water to his pigs, Hammack built a wooden trough above the mineral well and used its natural pressure to pump the water to the higher elevation. From there it was a simple matter of gravity and the principle that water seeks its own level to not only have running water to the pigs, but also to his nearby home. Eventually, he ran water to other downtown homes for $1 a month, though it was another decade before a non-mineralized sweetwater well provided more palatable liquid sustenance to downtown homes and businesses. All of Arlington relied on wells for water until the city built its own reservoir in 1957.

Though the flow has long since stopped, the mineral well head remains accessible on Center Street between the current day City Hall and the downtown municipal library.

And if the well wasn't enough to make 1892 a bad year for the city, things ended badly with Arlington's most famous feud—proof that ordinances aren't always sufficient to prevent violence or to close the gap between Old West style pioneer life and community security. A downtown shootout claimed four lives on Dec. 23, 1892, in an apparent dispute over a livestock deal gone sour. Casualties included "Poker" Bill Smith, J. Walker and George Hargrove and local cattleman Harvey Spears. A witness, as reprinted in a local paper on Christmas Eve the next day, gave the following account:

"Hargrove got word to Spear he was coming to get him. Told him what day and what train from Fort Worth. When he arrived, Spear was waiting at the depot. Poker Bill was on the right of way at the foot of Pecan Street. The three Hargroves were on the back of the train. Smith was killed when he raised his gun to fire. He was shot in the forehead. Spear killed George Hargrove and his father. Spear had been hit several times and his gun was empty. When Walker Hargrove approached him, Spear said, 'If I had one more bullet, I'd kill you too.' Walker shot Spear, turned and started walking down the railroad tracks toward Fort Worth. Bud Douglas, city marshal, started after him. Walker told him to go back or get the same."

Walker successfully claimed self-defense in court but eventually died himself in a saloon gunfight. One of the stray shots from the melee shot the horse from under a passing cowboy. Townspeople took up a collection and bought him a new horse.

Another development in Arlington attracted less headlines than the famous shootout but would ultimately be far more influential in the city's history. Citizen Edward Rankin had been a long-time advocate for public education and by 1894 his idea—to create a college—had picked up momentum. The idea was popular politically, so much so that L.M. Hammond and physician W.M Trimble promised to promote the possibility if they were elected to the town council, which they subsequently were. They donated $500 each and before long the college fund was up to $5,000, a princely sum at the time.

The idea caught fire. Merchants J.W. Ditto and A.W. Collins donated a block of land at the present site of the E.H. Hereford University Center on the UTA campus. Spruance and Rankin provided materials at cost. A brickyard operator threw in the bricks for a fireplace and foundation. The will to keep the college a local affair was so strong that when an out-of-town developer ended up with the low bid, Spruance took up a $100 collection to persuade the bidder to withdraw so that a local contractor could do the work.

The two-story frame structure, with outdoor privies and with water brought in from outside daily, opened as Arlington College in 1895 with William Trimble and Lee Hammond as principals. The building, which was used until the late 1930s, had six classrooms and an assembly room. The school opened with six teachers and around 100 students. It was not yet a college in a modern sense because elementary and secondary classes were part of the curriculum. The road ahead for the college would not be an easy one, either financially or in terms of identity. Its names and missions would change numerous times, but it would survive, eventually becoming the 35,000-student University of Texas at Arlington.

Like the college, Arlington itself would have many ups and downs of fortune and identity (what marketers today define as "brand") in the years after 1900. But developments in the final years of the 1800s would guarantee one thing: Arlington would always be at its very heart a college town.

Chapter 4 – 1900 to PV (pre-Vandergriff)

Arlington cannot boast that it bloomed in the first half of the 20th century, growth being steady but unremarkable, steadily inching upward from roughly 1,000 residents in 1900 to a census-estimated 7,800 in 1950. There were few clues in the decades following 1950 that Arlington would soon become one of the fastest growing cities in the country—indeed *THE* fastest growing for almost three decades. But it would take half a century before that particular boom became evident.

But that's not to say the 1900-1950 era wasn't interesting or colorful. The time frame was distinctly unique, so much so that Arlington could hardly be compared to the idyllic but ordinary "Our Town" popularized by Thornton Wilder's Pulitzer Prize winning play, a tale of average citizens in an average American hamlet. No doubt some of Arlington's residents were average but many of them, and the town, were not. The century may have started with the city looking like an average village, but before long Arlington would be known for several unusual attributes.

What the city did not escape was the same major economic, social and technological impacts that all U.S. cities experienced: World War I and World War II, the Great Depression, and sweeping changes in technology and communication that steadily shifted the nation from an agrarian society to one dominated by technology and science—the auto for the horse, the telephone and telegraph for the hand-written letter, mass manufacturing for hand crafting, the train, the plane and the bus for mass transit, movies and radio instead of live entertainment, the phonograph instead of the home piano. Modern medicine boomed with diagnostic and treatment innovations, while average life spans dramatically increased.

Every city was reborn, remade, sometimes created a new or sometimes destroyed in the wake of those changes and innovations, for better and for worse. The first half of the 20th century produced the most dramatic changes, in the fastest time, in the history of mankind. The question however, is this: What made Arlington unique at this time?

Consider first the question of physical form. Though originally surveyed as a half-mile square with hundred-yard blocks, in the 1900s, Arlington soon began shaping itself in a linear east-west geography that was primarily influenced by two factors. The first of those, arriving in 1902, was the Interurban, owned by the North Texas Traction Company. Essentially an electric trolley, the Interurban connected Dallas and Fort Worth through the middle of Arlington on Abram Street, which was then also a highway, with several stops in the city. Moving at speeds exceeding 50 mph, the Interurban sped up regional transportation and also made another phenomenon—the commuting resident—possible even in less dense urban environments like those in Texas.

The second major city shaper would begin evolving in the 1920s. U.S. 80, the famed Bankhead Highway, would run through Division Street in Arlington. It served for three decades as not only the chief connecting highway between Fort Worth and Dallas but also as a conduit for virtually all the East to West Coast traffic flows through the southern portion of the U.S., from Washington, D.C., to San Diego, Calif. The Bankhead preceded by decades both highway I-30, aka the Texas Turnpike, and I-20. As might be expected, much—really most—of Arlington's early commercial development took place along U.S.80, which for almost 30 years served as the city's main commercial "drag."

Institutions also affect a city, contributing to what in modern parlance would be considered a brand—an image with social, cultural and economic impacts.

For Arlington there were three specific entities that would have a profound impact on the city during the half century following 1900: the Berachah Industrial Home for the Redemption and Protection of Erring Girls; Arlington Downs (a horse racing track with legalized gambling) and the Top O'Hill Terrace Casino, a flourishing, highly illegal gambling enterprise that eventually gave Arlington the reputation of being a sort of early Las Vegas. Interestingly, the city voted itself dry in 1902, a condition that persisted well into the second half of the century.

Why not add the University of Texas at Arlington to this list of critical identifiers? Though its existence was no doubt significant, the college would struggle with economics, identity and enrollment in its early years, sometimes barely surviving. Its role would be highly amplified in the second half of the 20th century.

But what was Arlington like in the early 1900s? In 1904, Arlington Journal Editor William Stanberry summed up the city's status thusly: "The city contains 2,500 people, two banks, three gins, an oil mill, a $3,000 newspaper plant, a $15,000 school, a $20,000 military academy (a predecessor to UTA) with more than 100 cadets, four churches, a kindergarten, $30,000 worth of bricks built that year, four dry good stores, three drug stores, ten grocery stores, four hardware stores, one confectionary, one jeweler, four blacksmiths, one dentist, one lawyer, six doctors, two depots, rural mail delivery, an electric light and power plant, three lumber yards, one corn and flour mill, two corn shellers, three restaurants, one bakery, two livery stables, three furniture stores, a telephone system, steam and electric cars all day and night, two express companies, two barber shops, three meat markets, two hotels, one wagon yard and one dairy. The new school building contained seven large rooms, an office, an auditorium, sixteen cloak rooms and two large halls. Furnishings included desks of oak, blackboards, maps, charts, chemical apparatus and office furniture for the teachers."

Editor Stanberry alluded to the presence of the Texas and Pacific Train, which in those days also carried passengers, as well as the Interurban, this during an era in which the stage coach was still running. Historians later would note that Arlington—today the most populous city in the country without mass transit—in the early 1900s had three forms of such transit (passenger rail, the Interurban and stagecoach). Progress doesn't always share its bounty proportionally.

Few Arlington residents today are even aware of the impact that electric trolley systems had on the city's evolution.

The electric interurban industry in Texas totaled nearly 500 miles, the second largest interurban mileage among states west of the Mississippi River.

Interurban Electric Trolley

The Northern Texas Traction trolley system that served Dallas and Fort Worth, with Arlington in between, began operation in 1902 with 35 miles of track. Unlike the train, the service provided frequent passenger service between urban areas that could not be met by existing steam-railroad service. About 70 percent of the trolley lines in Texas were in the DFW area, with electric lines connecting Fort Worth and Cleburne, Fort Worth through Arlington to Dallas, and Denison, Dallas, Corsicana and Waco. The speed with which the electric trolleys could carry riders to their destinations was initially considered near-miraculous, all day journeys being transformed to an hour and what had been trips taking hours now taking minutes.

Though highly popular initially, the Interurban's business began to decline as improved highways were built, more modern and reliable vehicles were manufactured and private auto ownership became the vogue. The Interurban route between Dallas and Fort Worth was closed in 1934, with most of the rails eventually being removed for World War II use. Some of those rails, however, are said to still exist under Abram

Street near Arlington City Hall. The same generating system that powered the Interurban by day became a source of electric power for the city, that system eventually evolving into the current day Handley Power Plant that still exists at the intersection of Pioneer Parkway Boulevard and Loop 820 in Fort Worth.

Bankhead Highway (aka Division Street)

Though many political figures in Arlington's history have been happy to take credit for the city's booming growth, considerable credit must also be given to the luck of—Location. It is unlikely that anyone from Arlington, for instance, had much influence with good roads' promoter John Hollis Bankhead. Bankhead was a Confederate war hero and habitual politician who steadily worked his way up the political ladder from Alabama state representative to U.S. representative to U.S. senator. But the city benefited from Bankhead's vision anyway.

Bankhead Highway (Old Highway 80)

Bankhead was a staunch proponent of a southern highway continental route across the U.S., introducing legislation initially while he was in the House and then in the Senate, to improve roads and bridges. The Federal Road Act of 1916 formalized the continental route ambition. Though Bankhead died in 1920, the highway project named U.S. Highway 80, often carried his name. Given the proclivities of Congress it might have been possible for the project to wither, except that one of his sons, John

Hollis Bankhead II, was also elected to the Senate, as was a second son who became speaker of the House of Representatives, William B. Bankhead (father of actress Talullah Bankhead). All of the Bankheads in Congress steadfastly supported funding for U.S. 80, about seven miles of which eventually ran through the heart of Arlington.

Interstates 30 and 20 would later be described as "rivers of gold bringing growth and fortune to Arlington" by sociologist Paul Geisel, but initially it was U.S. 80 that kept Arlington from simply drying up as its economic structure based on farming faltered. Division Street/U.S. 80 developed restaurants, hotels and auto dealerships, for a while even being branded as the "Golden Arlington Auto Aisle." And, without the presence of highway access, two other entities of the era—Arlington Downs and Top O'Hill Terrace—would simply not have been possible.

Arlington Downs Racetrack

Arlington Downs

Though ranching and oil magnate William T. Waggoner was more known for owning one of the country's largest ranches near Vernon, Texas, he also owned a smaller 6,000-acre ranch between Dallas and Fort Worth, much of the acreage conveniently fronting U.S. 80, in Arlington known as East Division Street. As fortune would have it, the wealthy Waggoner—his obituary described him as the "the wealthiest man west of the Mississippi"—was a horse racing zealot of the best kind: the extremely wealthy kind.

Though pari-mutuel betting on horses was not then legal in Texas, in 1929 Waggoner built a 1.25 mile track with a 6,000-seat grandstand on his Arlington "Three-D" stock farm on the north side of Division Street between present-day Stadium Drive and Texas 360. The cost was then a staggering $3 million just as the nation was entering an extended depression. Waggoner hosted local civic events and prize races, quickly becoming popular with many local residents, while also spending freely on lobbying efforts at the state capital to legalize wagering.

Though gambling ostensibly did not take place, in 1931 a test case arose when two race-goers, J.B. Coulter and O. O. Franklin, were arrested at Arlington Downs for openly betting. The resulting publicity and court case allowed racing proponents to make their case public. In 1933 the Texas legislature legalized pari-mutuel betting. It issued the first permit (one of only two statewide) to a hastily remodeled Arlington Downs, which by then had been expanded to a capacity of 25,000, with another novelty. It was integrated, sort of, with whites on one side of the track and blacks on the other.

Waggoner's stated ambition was simple, if grandiosely appealing to Texans: He wanted a track and a race to rival those of the Triple Crown—for a Texas race to take its place with the Kentucky Derby.

The income generated by pari-mutuel betting breathed new life into the racetrack, and thoroughbred owners from across the country sent horses by rail to compete at Arlington Downs. During its first year of full operation under the new laws 650 horses ran on the track, profits averaged $113,731 a day, and the average daily attendance was 6,734. The track was a celebrity magnet, attracting stars like Will Rogers and even the Vice President of the United States, James Nance Garner.

The track would probably still be there today if not for a problem. Waggoner was already in his 80s and his health was steadily failing. In 1934 he died of a stroke, thus depriving the racing industry of one of its most vocal and affluent boosters.

In Austin, support was growing for repeal of pari-mutuel betting as pro-racing lobbyists scrambled to buy time. By careful maneuvering, a decision on the issue was avoided during the 1936–37 seasons, and the popularity and prestige of Arlington Downs grew throughout the country.

In 1937 the Texas Derby was heralded as being among the "tryouts" for the more famous Kentucky Derby.

But it was the Depression and Texas was in the Bible Belt. At the end of the 1937 regular session, despite the track's popularity and economic success, the state legislature repealed pari-mutuel laws. Arlington Downs was sold to commercial developers. The racetrack was used for rodeos, auto racing and other events, including an occasional movie and TV program location until 1958, when the buildings were razed. In 1978 a Texas historical marker was placed on the site.

Eventually in the 1950s the Three D stock farm would be sold to an up-and- coming developer named Angus Wynne. He would use the land and other property acquired around it to create the Great Southwest Industrial District—then one of the largest such projects in the country— and yet another entity that would become part of Arlington's future "Roller Coasters and Baseball" brand: Six Flags Over Texas Amusement Park.

The Top O'Hill Terrace Casino

Professional gamblers Benny "Cowboy" Binion and Fred Browning were not scholars but nevertheless they had an interesting economic hypothesis, which was this: If a lot of serious money was showing up in Arlington to bet on the ponies during the day, those same deep pockets would like to gamble at night when the track wasn't operating.

They were right. Thus it was that long before Las Vegas developed as the nation's gambling Mecca, the Top O'Hill Terrace was considered a luxury gaming establishment, though the facility didn't begin with that intention. Initially the structure, an upscale dining establishment built by Beulah Marshall, was located just outside the city's western city limits. It sat atop a hill with a view that stretched for miles, a restaurant accessible by automobile, thanks to the newly paved Bankhead Highway.

Top O'Hill Terrace Casino

Fort Worth gambler Fred Browning meanwhile had grown weary of moving his operation from hotel to hotel. He wanted a permanent establishment and he evidently had enough influence with assorted legal and political figures to stay out of harm's way.

Historian Leslie Wagner recounted events that followed in a Dallas History Examiner article.

"In 1926, Fred Browning of Fort Worth purchased the property and quickly began unusual renovations, moving the tearoom structure from its foundations to excavate for a basement double the size of the tearoom to serve as an underground gambling casino and then returned the structure to its original spot," she wrote. "Patrons turned off the highway down a 900-foot driveway to a large parking lot behind the building. At the peak of its popularity, customers exhausted a quarter million dollars on a weekend of gaming at the slot machines, crap and black jack tables, and roulette wheels. A brothel was also operated on the grounds along with the casino."

Though the casino was raided on occasion, Browning and Binion appeared to have knowledge of such events before they occurred. They had constructed an "escape" tunnel from the casino that led to a terraced tea garden. The casino also had secret hidden rooms in which gambling equipment could quickly be stashed.

A former employee at the casino, Jack Poe, said he met many celebrities at the casino, including some with notorious reputations— Clyde Barrow and Bonnie Parker being the most prominent. Browning required the pair to not bring their guns, Poe said.

The casino did not operate completely without public awareness or criticism, most notably that of Fort Worth firebrand preacher J. Frank Norris. He often railed about the casino from both the pulpit and his radio show. Norris' lamentations eventually reached the state level, the casino being successfully raided—"success" being defined as gambling equipment found and people arrested—in 1947 under the leadership of Texas Ranger Capt. M.T. "Lone Wolf" Gonzaullas. When a federal grand jury began investigating the casino in 1949 it was closed, Binion reportedly using his earnings to build the Horseshoe Casino in Las Vegas.

In one of those flukes of history, Norris' Bible Baptist Seminary bought the property in 1956 after both Browning and Norris had died. The property is now Arlington Baptist College and the statue that greets visitors to the grounds is that of Norris—not Browning or Binion. Both the escape tunnel and the tea garden still exist.

Berachah Industrial Home for the Redemption and Protection of Erring Girls

The definition for "Berachah" is as an acronym for "blessing," which was exactly the intent of the home's founder, the Rev. James T. Upchurch, who established the home on South Cooper Street in 1903. The area is currently part of UT Arlington and Doug Russell Park.

Upchurch, a Nazarene minister, originally established the Berachah Rescue Society in Waco in 1894, the idea being to aid "fallen" women, a controversial idea at the time. In 1903 he and his wife Maggie purchased 27 acres in Arlington to be used for the establishment of the Berachah

Home for homeless, unmarried, usually pregnant girls. The acreage included a slight rise that was promptly dubbed "Rescue Hill."

Berachah Home

Typically the girls showed up on the train or Interurban, coming from Texas and others states to have their babies and learn to care for themselves. Reportedly, adoption was not allowed because Upchurch believed children and their mothers should not be separated.

Over the next three decades the home expanded to include 40 more acres, including a hospital/clinic, nursery, dormitory and dining room named Hammil Hall, printing shop, handkerchief factory, chapel, office building, schoolhouse, auditorium, barn, and a cemetery. The girls were kept busy working in the printing shop, gardening, operating the handkerchief factory, teaching at the school and working at the hospital/clinic. Area churches and businessmen financially supported the home.

The home closed in 1935 for reasons not clearly known, but perhaps due to competition from the Edna Gladney Home in Fort Worth, or because of Reverend Upchurch's poor health. It was reopened later that year as an orphanage, the Berachah Child Institute, by Reverend Upchurch's daughter, Allie Mae, and her husband, the Rev. Frank Wiese. In 1942 the property was purchased by the Christian Missionary Alliance. The university purchased the property in 1963. The only visible sign of the Berachah Home today is a small cemetery just west of Davis Hall on the UT Arlington campus. Several babies and a few employees of the home are buried there, most being the victims of an influenza epidemic or childhood birth problems.

The records for the Berachah Home are kept in the Special Collections at the UT Arlington Library.

By 1950 the transitions for Arlington had been dramatic—probably more so than for most similar size communities. In just a few decades the city evolved from an agrarian, pioneer economy and went through two world wars and a depression. Meanwhile it gained and then lost a booming business in Arlington Downs. Then gained and lost the Top O'Hill Casino. Then gained—and lost—the Berachah Home. Meanwhile, the future University of Texas at Arlington had struggled along, remaining a two-year vocational college, by then called North Texas Agricultural College. It was a city, from a public relations perspective, with no brand of its own.

Though the Arlington Independent School District had been created in 1902, numerous small districts still remained, including the Johnson Station and Pantego schools. Both Dalworthington Gardens and Pantego existed, but as communities as opposed to incorporated cities.

Though Arlington had finally made something out of its problems with its mineral water—Epson salts like "Arlington Crystals" being sold prominently on drug store shelves—that business was about to go away. While the town no longer appeared to be "a few shacks on the prairie" as one traveler had once described it, Arlington appeared to be going no place and most certainly seemed in no particularly big hurry to get there. Though older than either Fort Worth or Dallas, both of those cities by 1950 had long since overshadowed Arlington both economically and politically. Even neighboring Grand Prairie, by then a rival of major proportions, appeared to be thriving in comparison. While the Texas and Pacific still went through town it rarely stopped, zipping through so quickly and sometimes lethally, that the intersection of Division and

Abram Streets and Fielder Road was dubbed "Death's Crossing."

To sum it up in 1950, it appeared that Arlington's best days were behind it. This assessment, however, turned out to be highly inaccurate. In retrospect it was more like the city was drawing a big breath before lunging into the second half of the century. It would do so launched by two powerful trends.

If the first half of the 1900s was marked by the departure of country folk to the big cities, the second half would be characterized by a march from big cities to the suburbs. Hundreds of thousands of once-upon-a-time soldiers were returning to civilian life. They wanted families and homes and schools—homes with garages and a place for that shiny car or maybe even two shiny cars. Commuting 30 or 40 minutes was rapidly becoming commonplace. By the thousands they began looking for opportunities, searching for a place to live that would offer them both the coveted suburban lifestyle and easy access to jobs in places like Dallas or Fort Worth.

A great many of them found it in Arlington, conveniently located halfway in the middle of DFW, right in the middle of the future Metroplex. At first, they didn't find the housing they needed, but there were those leaders who did see the future—who saw that a place in the middle of everything could be good not only for homes but for business as well. As it turned out, 1950 really was not so much the end of an era but the beginning of a new kind of life in America—the blended work-live-play style of suburbia that would eventually make Arlington a national phenomenon. The only missing ingredient was the appropriate kind of leadership and direction—a leadership that was just around the proverbial corner.

Chapter 5 – The Growth Years

Most Arlington residents from 1950 until the present didn't realize as much, but they were living within a remarkable phenomenon. Their hometown was a city that was shape shifting, reinventing itself year by year. Populations of many urban American cities have grown or shrunk a bit over the past century, but places like Pittsburgh or St. Louis were major cities in 1900 as they are today, though for some of them perhaps a little less so.

But Arlington does not have that kind of history. It was a hamlet of 1,000 in 1900, barely more than a village. Though it went through several transformations over the half century from 1900, by 1950 the city barely managed to grow to 7,800 people, making it just another pleasant little town, another rest stop between Fort Worth and Dallas.

But flash forward to today and Arlington's population, closing on 400,000, exceeds both the aforementioned St. Louis and Pittsburgh, making Arlington one of the nations 50 most populous cities. That's without a seaport or mountain vistas to attract visitors. Without mining or oil or other traditional natural resources. Without Fortune 500 corporate headquarters or the other amenities that typically make big cities become exactly that—big cities.

How can that happen? The answer is that Arlington became one of America's boom towns in tandem with a phenomenon that took place across the country—a phenomenon associated with a handy location, an unusually accomplished level of long-lasting, innovative leadership and more than a few lucky breaks.

That phenomenon? If the first half of the 20th century was characterized by people leaving the farms to live in the big cities, the second half was made notable by their leaving big cities to live in the suburbs. Much was made of the fact that Bill Clinton was the nation's first president to preside over a nation that had more people living in suburban areas than big cities. The suburban trend was, in fact, a human population shift tsunami.

"Crabgrass Frontier" author Kenneth Jackson conducted one of the first definitive studies of how "the good life" in America came to be equated with a home, two cars in the garage and a grassy yard, all located a reasonable commuting distance away from the urban workplace. Better roads, cheap fossil fuels, inexpensive land and economical building methods—and that grassy yard—made the "burbs" both attractive and economically attainable. This was aided in no small part by the obvious deterioration of many central cities. People, many of whom clearly disliked the high population density of their urban environments, bailed out to suburbia, first by the hundreds of thousands. Then by the millions.

One of the truths espoused by urban sociologists is that jobs and business will follow rooftops, eventually moving out of the inner city to the suburbs. The most affluent of such cities tend originally to have mostly Caucasian populations but steadily become more demographically diverse.

Jackson says such "fringe areas" increasingly take on urban characteristics. Like anything that's overdone, there were and continue to be unintended not-so-pleasant consequences of suburbanization: traffic, pollution related to high numbers of autos and isolation. A sense of community often takes a while to develop in suburbs. Other issues include urban decline, white flight, franchise store overpopulation, low-end apartments and other metropolitan problems. Also, suburban cities themselves often don't have the density to support cultural and mass transit entities. Too, in the process of growing, they often lose the smallish downtowns and businesses that were once endearing or at least sentimental characteristics.

Another urbanist, "Edge City" author Joel Garreau, divided suburbs into two major categories. The first was the traditional, commuting suburban community in which only a small percentage of the working population actually both lived and worked, sometimes with less than 10 percent working in the city in which they live (Colleyville, Keller or Mansfield would be good examples in Tarrant County).

The second type—a category in which Arlington clearly belongs—is Garreau's "edge city." Such a community, while still containing a high percentage of commuters, also has many jobs, offices, retail and often industry—a place where people live, work and shop that is not all that different from a traditional urban environment, albeit with continued reliance on the automobile and a less dense population per square mile.

Another phenomenon, Garreau said, also contributed to creation of edge cities like Arlington—working women, more specifically jobs for women. He points out that such cities began to take off in the late '70s, which was also the peak decade in all American history for women entering the work force. Indeed, in both the 1970s and 1980s, Arlington was the fastest growing city in the nation.

Despite the suburbanization ground swell, the reality is that there are many thousands of communities located near urban cities that may or may not have grown since 1950. But few can match the edge city growth dynamics of Arlington, where clearly all those factors that contribute to edge city development were present. Those include minutes away proximity (translating to a quick commute) to both Dallas and Fort Worth, the continued presence of freight rail, a couple of interstates, a four-year university, a nearby international airport and—probably most importantly—a sustained level of development-oriented leadership that stayed in place for more than a quarter century.

When opportunity, a national trend line and the appropriate energized and charismatic leadership show up at the same time, powerful dynamics can result. Arlington in the early 1950s was poised to take advantage of both the suburban growth and its location when the leadership showed up in the form of a 25-year-old would-be broadcaster named Tom Vandergriff.

Vandergriff, the son of Arlington Chevrolet and Buick dealer, W.T. "Hooker" Vandergriff, had attended the University of Southern California with ambitions of becoming a broadcaster.

Tom Vandergriff

Though slight in physical stature, Vandergriff possessed an impressive baritone and perfect diction with no trace whatsoever of a Texas or Southern accent. When he didn't land a broadcast job he returned home to work in the family business, a business that apparently ran well enough and profitably enough that the young Vandergriff had time on his hands. In 1949, despite being only 23, he was elected president of the local chamber of commerce, during which time Tom and his father discovered that General Motors was contemplating building a plant in the South, perhaps in Texas. Though most economists would consider the possibility of a small town like Arlington attracting a manufacturing plant that would provide more jobs than the entire town currently offered ludicrous, the Vandergriffs used their status as dealership owners to open a dialogue with the big auto maker. In 1951, Tom Vandergriff decided to make a run for mayor, hoping that GM would consider having such a friend in a position of power would seal the assembly plant deal.

No one is more a student of Arlington's growth than UT Arlington political science professor Allan Saxe, the author of the book "From Vandergriff to Greene: an Era of Continuity and Growth."

"Tom Vandergriff became mayor by challenging the incumbent mayor at the time, B.C. Barnes," Saxe said. "The election would become pivotal in the city's history. Vandergriff was elected mayor in April and in the summer of that year General Motors made its decision to come to Arlington."

The announcement that tiny Arlington would be the site of a giant auto plant shook the status quo of the region, rocking the city out of relative obscurity while attracting the attention of other potential investors and residents. Almost immediately the city became doubly attractive as not only a potential site for one of those new homes with a lawn but also for employment. Compared to most other blue collar endeavors in Texas at the time, GM assembly line jobs paid handsomely with attractive benefits.

"In 1954 the new assembly plant opened," Saxe wrote in his book. "It would signal the path that Arlington politics would take in the coming decades. A path of growth and development. During the next decade alone, Arlington's population would increase six-fold, to more than 49,000 residents by 1960."

Vandergriff, dubbed by political pundits as "the boy mayor," would remain in office for more than a quarter-century, also serving as one of the creators and presidents of the North Texas Council of Governments, all the while pursuing a relentless strategy of growth and annexations that would ultimately change the city from its original half-mile square to almost a hundred square miles.

The list of Vandergriff's achievements during his 26 years as mayor was impressive. He also acquired land to build Lake Arlington, which, despite being labeled "Vandergriff's folly" by critics, filled up in a single monsoon-like month in 1957. This was a critical advancement because the projected future water use by GM alone exceeded the capability of all of Arlington's well system at the time.

The mayor's welcoming attitude to new development along with the national attention the city was receiving attracted other investors. One of those was Dallas businessman Angus Wynne, who had purchased W.T. Waggoner's old ranch and other surrounding property, with an eye to building the Great Southwest Industrial District, at the time one of the nations largest such projects. When Wynne ran into economic difficulties, a brainstorming session between Wynne, Vandergriff and other GSID participants came up with a funding mechanism idea. The concept was a Disneyland-type attraction dubbed Six Flags over Texas, a reference to the six flags that had flown over the state. The park opened in 1961 and quickly evolved into the state's top commercial tourist attraction.

Vandergriff quickly determined that the Bankhead Highway, U.S. 80, simply wasn't going to be adequate for the city's transportation access needs. He became an advocate for a paid toll road connecting Dallas to Fort Worth, through Arlington of course, pledging to voters that when bonds for the roadway were paid off, it would become a free road.

The newly created Texas Turnpike Authority would begin construction of the state's first toll road, the Dallas-Fort Worth Turnpike, in 1955 and would open the road in 1957. Fee or not, the Turnpike avoided more than 80 stoplights on the U.S. 80 route between the two big cities. Traffic boomed, so much so that bonds were paid off 17 years ahead of schedule in 1977. Though toll road advocates tried to keep the tolls on the road to pay for other possible road projects in the region, Vandergriff was insistent: The promise had been that the road would be free when its debt was eliminated, and such became the case. The Turnpike became Interstate 30.

The downside? U.S. 80, Division Street in Arlington, began a slow deterioration as it lost traffic to I-30 and I-20, a process that has not substantially diminished over the years. Leadership hopes the presence of the Dallas Cowboys and Texas Rangers and resurgence in downtown development will positively affect Division Street's commercial viability.

The Turnpike fed Arlington's suburban housing explosion and contributed to the success of Six Flags and the industrial district. Not content with I-30, Vandergriff also lobbied for a second interstate route through the city, I-20; a route that was completed in the 1980s after Vandergriff had left office. Its economic impact in terms of attracting amenities such as The Parks Mall and the Highlands—as well as kicking off development in the southern section of the city—cannot be overstated and continues today.

Vandergriff's mayoral tenure included creation of the city's first real hospital, Arlington Memorial. Vandergriff also saw long-lasting rivalries such as those between Dallas and Fort Worth (or between Arlington and Grand Prairie) as often being counterproductive. As literally the mayor in the middle, he became an advocate of regionalism, helping to lead the way toward creation of the North Texas Council of Governments (COG) in 1966, serving as the first president. As president of the North Texas Commission, a sort of regional business advocacy group, Vandergriff introduced the world "Metroplex" as a synonym for the entire region. It caught on.

"He was criticized in the early days of COG by people who said we were going to create a new layer of government, and local members would lose their identity," said Michael Morris, transportation director for COG. "But look what's happened. He put together a group of people that every day worried about the region and created a partnership."

No stranger to lobbying, Vandergriff first successfully advocated the transition of Arlington State College into a four-year institution with the Texas A&M System. When A&M leadership did not—in Vandergriff's view—provide sufficient support, he lobbied successfully for a transition to the University of Texas system in 1967, creating today's University of Texas at Arlington, now with an enrollment exceeding 35,000.

"I don't consider what happened in Arlington as a personal achievement," Vandergriff said in a reflective Star-Telegram article. "It was an era when, for example, if we needed a hospital we could build it, or if we had to have a lake for our water supply we constructed it. If we wanted our junior college to become a university, we had the ability to see that it was done. In other words, a spirit developed that if we as a community wanted something strongly enough, we could reach that goal. During those years a feeling emerged that anything was within our reach if we wanted to attain it."

Sometimes the "anything was within our reach" attitude seemed overly optimistic, such as attracting a Major League Baseball team, but both the attitude and persistence somehow paid off.

Indeed, it was baseball that made Vandergriff a nationally prominent figure. His original idea that suburban Arlington—with access to all the people in the Metroplex—would make an ideal home for a Major League Baseball team, was a possibility roundly scoffed at initially. Nevertheless, he doggedly began a 13-year effort to bring a team to Arlington. The city already had Turnpike Stadium, which over the years had been home for a couple of minor league teams. In 1971, Vandergriff persuaded the woeful and deeply-in-debt Washington Senators, owned by Bob Short, to move to Arlington, despite pleas from baseball fans and President Richard Nixon to keep the team in the nation's capital.

The team became the Texas Rangers, playing in a quickly revamped and expanded, mostly metal, Arlington Stadium. Vandergriff himself served as one of the TV broadcast anchors. He threw out the first pitch at the Rangers' inaugural game on April 21, 1972, and in 2010 saw the team advance to its first World Series. Vandergriff died soon after in 2010. After his 26-year mayoral stint, he served a single term as a U.S congressman followed by several terms as Tarrant County commissioners' court judge. The city had been barely a square mile and 3,500 people when he had showed up as a 2-year-old boy in the city in 1929. Both its area and population increased more than a hundred-fold during his lifetime, much of which should be credited to his efforts.

Did Vandergriff succeed at everything? Or most? Like baseball, nobody in politics has a lifetime 1,000 average. The taxpayer-financed

Seven Seas Sea Life Park, which featured a high-flying killer whale named Newtka, along with performing dolphins and penguins on roller skates, opened near Arlington Stadium in 1972. Though the startup was initially successful, the decision not to offer rides so as not to compete with Six Flags next door proved to be a poor business decision. The park was closed after four years and the site currently hosts both the Sheraton Hotel and Arlington Convention Center. In later years another major tourist attraction, now called Hurricane Harbor, would feature a multitude of water-oriented rides and amenities but no animal acts at all.

Also, an effort to provide an Arlington location for the Texas College of Osteopathic Medicine failed when it was opposed by the M.D. community, in retrospect a grievous error. The college is now located in Fort Worth and is part of the University of North Texas system.

And though Vandergriff endorsed the idea of a mass transit system serving Arlington, voters turned the proposal down—as they did for the two mass transit elections after his mayoral tenure. Arlington today remains the only city among the nation's 100 most populous communities that does not have mass transit.

Too, Vandergriff's Anaheim-style vision for Arlington—a series of commercial and governmental service clusters surrounded by housing projects as opposed to a traditional downtown—was a commercial success but played havoc with maintaining the city's small but historic downtown.

In baseball parlance, Vandergriff would have been hitting about .800—an astronomic rate of success. If a hall of fame for mayors existed, he'd certainly be among its members. His successes far outnumbered his setbacks. That kind of track record would be difficult for Vandergriff's successors. Vandergriff resigned in January of 1977, allowing the appointment of Mayor Pro Tem S.J. Stovall, an engineer with the Army Corps of Engineers, to the office. Stovall was originally elected to the council in 1963. He served three terms as mayor until 1983; his successor being another councilman, banker Harold Patterson.

Though both Stovall and Patterson provided stable leadership, city politics clearly became more volatile after Vandergriff's departure. Council members or candidates like Sam Hamlett, Martha Walker—the city's first woman councilmember—Jim Norwood, Dick Malec, Roy "Skippy" Brown, Lico Reyes, Leo Berman and Gary Bruner often engaged in spirited, often-rancorous political contests sometimes involving non-traditional topics such as homosexuality portrayals in community theater and off-color book stores or other sexually oriented entertainment such as topless bars. The council became more of a partisan political environment as Arlington—like many affluent suburbs—transitioned from a Democratic to Republican-dominated environment, often mixed with Libertarian overtones. Some council members, like Malec, also attacked the traditional role of the city manager and other municipal practices such as a reliance on expensive consultants.

UTA political scientist Allan Saxe—himself an unsuccessful council candidate—saw a positive to the suddenly heated Arlington political environment. "Some have described these individuals as political mavericks, dissenters or naysayers," Saxe said. "But the fabric of democracy needs a variety of people to poke, probe and bother those in power, invoking different points of view in the mix. Vandergriff presided over a much more homogeneous community."

When financial executive Richard Greene was elected mayor in 1987 he already had two terms as a councilman as well as experience on the Planning and Zoning Commission. Though often considered a Vandergriff protégé, he inherited a full-blown edge city with an increasingly diverse population. It was, by then, Saxe said, "a mature city" that could no longer be run in the paternalistic fashion of the Vandergriff years.

Greene would remain mayor for a decade until 1997. Though he did not have the financial freedom to dedicate all his free hours to governance as Vandergriff did, he nevertheless donated massive amounts of his energy, considerable talents and intellect to manage a rapidly growing town that was being challenged for economic development assets.

"Tom Vandergriff brought the General Motors plant to Arlington, but it would be Richard Greene who would help keep it there," Saxe said. "Vandergriff brought Major League Baseball to Arlington, but it would be the leadership of Greene that kept it here."

When competing cities in the Dallas-Fort Worth area—and cities outside Texas as well—attempted to convince the Texas Rangers baseball club to leave Arlington, Green developed a winning plan to build a new ballpark. The ballpark would be paid for in part by a sales tax levy approved in a record and overwhelmingly favorable local election turnout that came despite sometimes virulent opposition from those opposing the venture. The success of the ballpark project eventually had state and national repercussions as well. The managing partner of the Texas Rangers at the time was George W. Bush, who—it could be argued—used the success and focus on his Rangers involvement to first catapult himself into the Texas governorship and eventually to the presidency. The new baseball facility, called The Ballpark in Arlington, opened in 1994 and hosted the MLB All-Star Game in 1995.

Greene was also at the helm in the early 1990s when GM put the Arlington plant on the list for possible closure. The mayor put together a coalition of state, national and regional proponents—sugared with tax concessions and an accommodating union—and convinced the big auto maker to stay in Arlington.

Greene also expanded public safety and the pace of city street repairs, as well as supporting creation of the massive 1,300-acre River Legacy Parks on the Trinity River and a Nature Center built primarily with private contributions. Despite heavy criticism from some quarters he also pioneered the idea of limiting smoking in public places, the success of which prompted a wave of municipal replications throughout the region that continues today.

I-20, originally envisioned as a high tech corridor, began a development boom during Greene's tenure that continues in the modern era, albeit dominated by retail, restaurants and auto dealerships.

Arlington, already a college town, became even more so when voters—with Greene's support and endorsement—approved funding of a Tarrant County College campus in the city. The new campus opened in 1995 with 5,000 students—maximum capacity. The Southeast campus continued to grow rapidly and in 2011 had an enrollment of almost 15,000 for-credit students.

The verdict for Greene?

"His tenure of office can be compared favorably with that of Vandergriff," Saxe said. "Vandergriff's tenure was much longer as mayor, but at a different time. In 1993, the CATO Institute, a respected think tank, recognized Arlington as the best professionally run city in the country. That was a remarkable achievement."

Greene's replacement as mayor was Elzie Odom, the first-ever African-American councilmember or mayor. Like Greene, he had also served on the Planning and Zoning Commission. As a council member, Odom focused on mobility, transportation and economic development issues, continuing those efforts as a three-term mayor. He was mayor when the city paid off its ballpark debt in 2001, nearly 10 years ahead of schedule.

Odom endorsed a sales tax program to increase funding for street maintenance, an idea that was subsequently approved by voters in 2002. City appointments under his tenure increasingly reflected the city's growing diversity, with Odom working with Asian, Hispanic and African American organizations. Though he left office in 2003, he later chaired a successful effort to ensure participation of minority and women-owned businesses in the $1.2 billion Cowboys Stadium.

The mayoral successor to Odom was Dr. Robert Cluck, a popular local obstetrician-gynecologist whose political career began in an unusual way, with an almost-fatal motorcycle accident that impaired the physician's arm strength and coordination. The long recovery and rehabilitation gave Cluck time to think about political involvement and—when he finally decided to run for office—he prevailed over incumbent Joe Ewen, who many had considered the heir-apparent to Greene.

Cluck served two terms as a councilman, tossing his hat into the mayoral race when Greene did not seek re-election, winning the post in 2003 in the midst of an evolving national economic downturn that included a myriad of issues including diminished sales tax revenues, lowered property valuations and higher expenses of government because of factors like medical costs and medically-related pension benefits. He quickly became an advocate for air quality improvements and other environmental considerations while consistently resisting the implementation of higher city taxes.

Privatization of the city's landfill provided one economic bonanza for the city, but another city windfall during Cluck's tenure was one that could not have been predicted —a natural gas bonanza beneath the city's surface. With thousands of acres in parks and other land holdings the city found a multi-million dollar cash source. The council earmarked half of the proceeds for the general fund and half diverted to a non-profit Tomorrow Foundation that funded and continues to fund a variety of cultural and human service grants. Cluck was an early supporter of the Levitt Pavilion, a downtown Arlington outdoor space that provides more than 50 free concerts a year and which has become a flagship for the city's cultural efforts as well as a symbol of a redeveloping downtown.

Those considerable accomplishments aside, Cluck's claim to fame will always hinge on another accomplishment: He brought the National Football League Dallas Cowboys to Arlington.

Cowboys' owner Jerry Jones had for years made no secret of his unhappiness with Texas Stadium in Irving. He said the facility was too small, susceptible to snits of bad weather and couldn't accommodate the luxury suites that Jones wanted. Nor did it have the capacity to accommodate the massive events that Jones had in mind, such as major concerts or events like the National Basketball Association All-Star Game, Final-Four tournaments, bowl games, Olympics or—the mother lode bonanza of major events in this country—the Super Bowl.

Naturally, Jones wanted major government support for the new facility, which Irving did not show an inclination to fund. Likewise, when Jones talked to Dallas leaders like then-Mayor Laura Miller or County Commissioner John Wiley Price he found both criticism and a reluctance to ante up to a half-billion dollar share of the new facility.

There was, however, one viable alternative—one city in the region that had enough cap room within its sales tax structure to help fund a facility, which by then Jones had scaled back to $650 million. Before Cluck, Mayor Odom had discussions with the Cowboys owner regarding the stadium but most pundits believed the talks were no more than attempts to soften the ground for negotiations with Dallas. Perhaps they began that way, but that wasn't the way they ended.

Cluck recalls a pivotal conversation with the volatile Jones in which the owner laid out the $650 million figure.

"I told him we were good for half of it, but absolutely no more than half of it," Cluck recalled telling Jones, in retrospect a bold and perhaps politically reckless commitment. The ultimate call would have to be made by voters. And not in a local election. The election would be held on Nov. 2, 2004—a national election day. Though early public opinion surveys had indicated less than enthusiastic support, that viewpoint shifted by election day. Some 111,000 voters showed up, with slightly more than 55 percent endorsing financial support of the stadium, which involved a mix of sales, hotel and rental car taxes along with ticket and parking taxes.

Star-Telegram columnist Gil Lebreton labeled it "A victory, yes, for owner Jerry Jones and all that you might think of him. But more than that, it was a triumph for a community that continues to believe it's a big league city, a city that continues to think, 'Yes,' while others around it say 'No.'"

Meanwhile a Dallas Morning News editorial read: "Chalk up one big missed opportunity for Dallas…Leaders have again squandered a once-in-a-generation opportunity to return the team to the city that bears its name."

Though the city's share remained at the maximum $325 million, Jones ultimately spent an estimated $1.2 billion for the stadium, currently valued at $1.5 billion, for the NFL's largest venue; a dazzling indoor stadium that includes a $40 million high-definition video board and the world's largest retractable glass doors, 120-foot high and 180-foot wide.

Jones waxed ecstatic when the stadium opened in May of 2009. "I really will say that, to think the Cowboys fans of the past will feel good about this place, as well as the ones in the future, that to me is what it ought to be about relative to the stadium," he said. "That is the incentive I had to go ahead to do some things I'm doing relative to the 'wow factor.' We will not only benefit, but it's going to make everybody who ever has had anything to do with this team proud."

The potential of the stadium was immediately obvious. The first summer the stadium hosted a variety of shows, from a Jonas Brothers concert to international soccer matches. In future months and years it would host some of our nation's eminent sporting events: Super Bowl XLV, the 2009 Big XII Football Championship and Cotton Bowl, the 2010 NBA All-Star Game and the 2014 men's Final Four. Forbes Magazine listed the team as the most valuable sports franchise in the U.S. and the second most valuable in the world.

Arlington received other benefits related to the Cowboys' presence, those being major improvements to I-30 interchanges, as well as to Texas 360, the economic repercussions of which will no doubt be long lasting. The presence of the Cowboys in Arlington will be Cluck's legacy long after he leaves office, though his administration did not end with the arrival of the Cowboys. He was easily re-elected in 2011.

Though many cities reinvent themselves over time, the changes in Arlington's image, size and "brand" were remarkable. What began in pioneer days as a simple farming community served by a railroad morphed in the early 1900s to a city known for both legal and illegal gambling, a smallish college, mineral waters and the Berachah Home.

Of those, only the college remained after 1951—the year the Main and Center streets mineral well was shut down. While the city's 1950s' and early 1960s' reputation focused on booming suburban housing and the blue collar presence of GM and the Great Southwest Industrial District, that image quickly changed to a more touristy tone with the arrival of Six Flags' roller coasters and Texas Rangers professional baseball, that being followed by the presence of the Dallas Cowboys. The city had also evolved into a college town of major proportions, with UT Arlington and TCC having a combined enrollment of more than 50,000, an asset that cannot and should not be underappreciated.

The 2010 census estimated Arlington's population at 365,438, up 9.8 percent from its 2000 number. This made the city's Texas' seventh most populous, ranking about 48th nationally. The city's growth was continuing, albeit at a slower pace than in previous decades, but much of that growth had a considerably different demographic dynamic. Arlington's 1970 population of just over 90,000 was about 90 percent Caucasian. The Arlington of 2010 had a white majority of 47.5 percent, the city's school district having already become a majority minority entity in the previous decade. Hispanic (27.4 percent) and Asian populations (6.7 percent) continued to boom, with the census indicating that 19 percent of the city's residents were born in another country. African Americans represented 18.4 percent of the population and Arlington's Vietnamese population ranked as one of the 15 most numerous in the country.

Economically the town was middle class with an average annual household income of just under $53,000, and it was also a young town in a nation that continued to age. The average age was 31.2, less than the state average of 33 and even younger than the overall county average.

Though voters generally—despite virulent opposition from some—favored proposals for major sports, voters were often not so agreeable when it came to other issues. From 1980 through 2011, the electorate rejected mass transit projects soundly on three occasions. A vast linear park project that would have created a remarkable linear, miles-long green zone along Johnson Creek in the middle of the city received a similar fate. Voters also turned down a funding proposal for a Smithsonian Museum affiliate. Arlington also appeared to be the first city in Texas to reject a sales tax-funded crime zone, and voters also initially balked at expanding tax limits for the Arlington school district.

Mark Twain once said that progress was good—unless it went on too long. In that vein, there were also those who lamented the loss of the Arlington that existed before its boom years.

"Texas Monthly" writer Gary Cartwright, who grew up in Arlington, waxed woefully as much in a 2005 article.

"Fifty years after I left Arlington, the quaint place I grew up in has been overrun by soulless neighborhoods, gridlocked streets, and a jumble of amusement parks and stadiums," Cartwright opined in one such "Texas Monthly" article. "This is progress? There was a time I could find my way around Arlington blindfolded. Downtown was a cozy little four-block span of turn-of-the-century stores and cafes, in easy walking distance from my home on Pecan Street. Cars were permitted to park down the middle of Main Street."

Cartwright, in eloquent if melancholy fashion, lamented the loss of a town so small a child could bike it easily and safely, along with the disappearance of non-franchise businesses like Terry Brother's Drug Store, Albert's Pool Hall and a host of town characters.

Cartwright clearly sympathizes with the "You Can't Go Home Again" sentiments of Thomas Wolfe, though the reality is that such nostalgia would likely be true for anyone visiting their hometown a half century after they left it.

Arlington by 2011 clearly seemed to be making progress in both revitalizing its downtown area and also in finally transforming its old city center into a blended communiversity in which residents and university students would mix—the sort of creative class-appealing environment advocated by urbanist Richard Florida. The combination of downtown revitalization featuring restaurants and cultural attractions and a growing resident student population boded well for an accelerating rebirth of the downtown area. It would be a downtown that Arlington Council member Lana Wolff predicted would quickly evolve into "everybody's neighborhood." But it would also still be, in 2012, a work in progress.

Chapter 6 – Pantego and Dalworthington Gardens

It is sometimes difficult for area newcomers to recognize when they've actually left Arlington and ventured into one of the two small cities surrounded by 100-square-mile Arlington: Pantego and Dalworthington Gardens. Though the markings on police cars change, street names that run through multiple jurisdictions generally do not. And though all three communities have a different set of elected government officials, all share the same public school district. If a Pantego or Dalworthington Gardens resident has a library card, it's probably for the Arlington system. Most likely, Pantegoites and "Gardeners" also share another characteristic with their Arlington neighbor. If they work, they probably commute outside the city.

Pantego checks in at a smidge under two square miles and just less than 2,400 residents, a number that hasn't changed much over the 2000 and 2010 census counts. Dalworthington Gardens is similar in land area—not quite two square miles –and also in population, about 2,300, though the town did grow a little, about 3 percent, over the past decade, while Pantego did not. Both cities also share other characteristics, such as a demographic that is mostly Anglo. Also, on average, its residents are older and more affluent than other citizens of Tarrant County or Texas. Additionally, both towns reside within the Eastern Cross Timbers geological stratum, which means sandy soils and a bounty of native oak trees. Pantego has a distinct commercial advantage with the help of two east-west roadways popular with retail business, Park Row and Pioneer Parkway.

For practical and cultural purposes the overlap between the communities and Arlington is substantial in terms of employment, civic, cultural and charitable organizations, schools, churches and other concerns. But historically, each is unique.

Pantego

Though Pantego traces its modern history from the 1880s, for much of the time it was an essentially rural, unincorporated community with a distinctly agrarian lifestyle. Its incorporation as an official municipality began as a stop-and-start, on-again, off-again process that included being briefly annexed and then dis-annexed by Arlington in the early 1950s in a conflict over lack of city services and the fact that some residents simply did not want to be either incorporated or be part of Arlington. As a Texas general law city (those of less than 5,000 population), Pantego has limited power to annex new territory while larger "home rule" Arlington does have that authority, over the years expanding around and surrounding Pantego.

Pantego Park

When it became clear that the Pantego area was eventually going to be part of some formal community, residents voted to incorporate—with minor later adjustments—in 1952. But the real history of the area begins much earlier, with the arrival of the man most historians consider the father of Pantego, Col. Frederick Forney Foscue, a native of North Carolina, born in 1819.

Foscue, like many Americans of that era, moved westward more than once. He was a state representative (1849—1851) and lawyer in Alabama before settling in Smith County, Texas, in 1853. A habitual politician, he was elected to the Texas Legislature, serving as a state representative and state senator intermittently from 1859 to 1866. He supported the Ordinance of Secession, one of the primers for the Civil War. He served in the Confederacy and was referred to as Colonel Foscue, though a colonel he may not have been. Surviving records of the

Confederacy list F. F. Foscue as a captain who served as enrolling officer in one of the Confederate Congressional Districts in East Texas

He could have been, but probably was not, promoted to a higher rank. An old Southern tradition seemed to be that anyone who served as a Civil War officer—and some enlisted men as well—ended up being called colonel for life. The Town of Pantego website also notes the possibility that Foscue was a member of a veterans group that perpetuated military titles in the hierarchy of the organization.

He married his first cousin, Mary Jane Foscue, who did not like Texas, perhaps sharing the sentiment from a widely circulated Texas pioneer housewife: "Texas is a heaven for men and dogs but hell for women and oxen."

She divorced the colonel and returned to Alabama, which seemed not to particularly bother Foscue. He married twice again, the last time to Mary Ann Floyd Foscue. It is uncertain when Foscue arrived in the area, but he began buying land in what would become the Pantego area after the Civil War, apparently aided somewhat by another colonel, Middleton Tate Johnson. An 1876 Tarrant County courthouse fire destroyed many transaction records, muddying clear distinctions of who bought what land at what time.

Too, some land titles in Tarrant County and much of the rest of North Texas were still in dispute during Foscue's era because of conflicts related to an 1841 impresario grant. It was made by the Republic of Texas to 20 American and English investors led by William Peters, an effort generally referred to in historical texts as the Peters Colony. Peters signed four different contracts with the Republic of Texas, each adding to the level of confusion over who owned what. The confusion increased when some of the Peters Colony stakeholders sold their rights, the validity of land claims growing more muddled when Texas joined the union, the inevitable litigation taking years to resolve.

The bottom line, though, was that the first Peters Colony homesteaders began arriving in the 1840s, typically receiving 640 acres per household or 320 for an individual.

Foscue used his skills as an attorney, banker and investor to buy and sometimes sell land and reportedly accumulated 3,360 acres in Tarrant, Jack and Scurry counties. Some of his land was apparently farmed by sharecroppers. He was a dominant figure in the settlement of the Pantego area and should be regarded as the first Pantego—and Arlington—land developer.

Where does the name "Pantego" come in? Tradition holds that Foscue had a loyal and trusted Caddo Indian friend named Pantego. When fellow tribesmen were moving to Indian Territory, the present day Oklahoma, Indians stopped at the Foscue plantation and demanded that Pantego accompany them or help them in some other way. Pantego refused and was murdered on the spot, supposedly by hanging. He and his wife and family were buried on what was then described as Briarwood Hill, currently near the northeast corner of Bowen Road at Park Row.

On December 20, 1883, Foscue donated one acre of his land in trust for school purposes. A one dollar nominal consideration was paid by the trustees of the Pantego school community. Tradition holds that the school was to be named Pantego in honor of Foscue's Indian friend. The Pantego School was eventually folded into the Arlington Independent School District system.

The word "Pantego" is said to be of Caddo origin and is loosely translated to "lying wolf" or "stalking wolf." There is, however, a Pantego, N.C., and a Pantego Creek in North Carolina—the state where Foscue grew up—though the similarities of the name might be coincidental.

Foscue continued to develop land in the Arlington area and became a well-known banker. He died at his home, reportedly after being bitten by a rabid skunk, on March 3, 1906. His remains have since been transferred to Parkdale Cemetery in Arlington.

The census numbers show Pantego to be a town of golden-years residents, many of whom are retired. The average age is almost 48 compared to neighboring Arlington's 31. The median household income has been decreasing slightly, one of two Tarrant County cities with that distinction.

A census snapshot of the town in 2010 is as follows:

Pantego Census Demographics 2010	
Population in 2000	2,394
2010 population	2,318
White, all ethnicities	89.7%
Hispanic	5%
Foreign-born	2.3%
18 and older	81%
Average family size	2.84
Mean retirement income	$24,636
Median monthly mortgage payment	$1,635
Mean commute time	21.9 minutes
Native Texans	62.4%

But the trend of being one of the area's residentially older communities may be ending, or so claimed former Pantego City Manager Doug Davis in a 2011 Star-Telegram article. Davis said he believes the pendulum is swinging back the other way.

"In the last few years, we've seen lots of younger people who grew up in Pantego moving back to town to raise their kids here," he said. "Some of them are moving into their parents' houses."

Pantego's small-town feel, city services and proximity to major cities are attractive, he said, but one of the biggest draws is the Arlington schools that serve the area: Hill Elementary, Bailey Junior High and Arlington High. Alumni are moving back so that their own children can attend, he said.

Mortgage figures support's Davis' perception. The number of purchases of existing homes by new owners is on the increase compared to the past decade. In 2000, 47.4 percent of residents had no mortgage, compared with 38.4 percent a decade later, an indication that many homes are now occupied by new owners.

But, the Star-Telegram article noted, almost 63 percent of the city's homes were built in the 1960s and '70s; only 2.2 percent were built since 2005. Thanks to major commercial arteries the city also enjoys higher sales tax revenue per capita than is typical for most small Texas communities and the city's infrastructure is well maintained. Though some undeveloped parts of the city remain, that area represents only a small percentage of the community. Full build-out is very near. City property taxes also remain low, in 2011 being 37.3 cents per $100 valuation, among the lowest in the county.

Dalworthington Gardens

Dalworthington Gardens has two claims to fame that few people recognize: First, it is the largest city in Texas. Or at least it is in the number of letters in its name, 21.

For the record, "Dalworthington" is a combination of portions of the names for Arlington, Dallas and Fort Worth.

And the "Gardens" part?

"The Garden part of the name was because the land was so fertile and it grew good vegetables," former Alderman Velma Bogart said, she also being a resident since 1974.

The second claim to fame? It's the only surviving municipality in a Depression-era subsistence city experiment that attempted to combine access to urban jobs and amenities with the ability to produce vegetables and fruits for home consumption. In effect, the attempt was to create tiny farms for low income residents who would also enjoy easy access to big cities like Dallas and Fort Worth. Typically those homesteads were anywhere from almost four to just over 24 acres.

Big lots—the minimum is a half-acre—and low city taxes has long been a mainstay of DWG, where the property tax rate in 2011 was a scant 26.3 cents per $100 valuation, the lowest of any municipality in Tarrant County, a seeming contradiction in that DWG's residents are also among the most affluent on a per household average basis.

"We're living that American dream–well above our dreams," DWG Police Chief Bill Waybourn said in a 2011 Star-Telegram article.

Background: If Middleton Tate Johnson was the father of Arlington and Tarrant County, and Frederick Foscue was the father of Pantego, it would be reasonable to conclude that Dalworthington Gardens also had a historical father of sorts. But in this scenario, the gender-correct phrase would be "mother," that being First Lady Eleanor Roosevelt.

Roosevelt had witnessed the wholesale departure of hundreds of thousands of Americans from farms and ranches during the Great Depression, a condition worsened by a drought in much of the country. The First Lady strongly believed in a "back to the land" movement and said as much to her husband, Franklin Roosevelt.

With presidential backing, Homestead Division Director and Public Works Administrator Milburn L. Wilson came up with the subsistence city program, envisioned as a means of freeing the industrial workers from the dreaded city. Despite presidential endorsement, the idea was not embraced by everyone. Secretary of the Interior Harold L. Ickes said he was "disappointed in certain aspects of the program" and called it the "biggest headache of his career." Also, Resettlement Administration Director Rexford Tugwell in his memoirs noted that he "had reservations about the entire homestead idea."

Why the Dalworthington Gardens location? Herbert Antley, in a 1980 master's thesis for UT Arlington (Dalworthington Gardens: A New Experiment in Planned Utopia) noted that the Roosevelt's son, Elliot, became engaged to a woman from the local area in July of 1933.

"Elliot and his mother were invited to visit in the home of Elliot's friend, Carl Mosig, the Fort Worth Bureau chief of the Dallas Morning News, who lived near Arlington, Texas," Antley noted in his thesis. "During this visit, Eleanor saw the possibilities for a homestead on the land across the street and passed her idea on to those who were investigating sites for the projects across the country."

As is usually the case in such matters, the First's Lady's suggestion was taken seriously, and thus it was that a federal inspection of land south of a dusty and unpaved section of Arkansas Lane became the site for one of five experimental subsistence cities across the country. The federal government allotted $250,000 to buy 593.3 acres, within which would be 80 sites for development of land south of Arkansas Lane near Arlington, Texas. Applications from potential homeowners soon began trickling in. The new community had six dirt roads, three running north-south and three east-west.

Early Dalworthington Gardens Home

"When applicants moved into the homes, there were no garages, no fences, no driveways, no paved roads," Antley's thesis research reported. "Butane gas was furnished later, but initially only wood or coal could be used to heat the homes and cook the meals. Family and neighbors had to help rescue automobiles from the mud during heavy rains. Because the building of fences in the project was delayed until 1937, it was rather difficult to raise livestock on the premises. Many homesteaders already owned cows, chickens, and pigs, and they brought them along to their new homes. The roaming around of these animals and subsequent herding back to their owners was a common sight in the gardens before the fences were built."

The government's low bidder strategy tended to create other issues related to substandard electricity and carpentry problems. A flawed sewage system also resulted in many residents having to build their own septic tank systems. And if that wasn't problem enough, a contractor hired to build a pipeline from nearby water well brought in lines that had previously been used in an oil field, not ideal for what was supposed to be drinkable water.

Nor did the "Gardens" part of the city's name live up to expectations.

One resident complained in a Fort Worth Press article, "I'll have to pasture most of it two or three years before I can raise a crop." The sandy soil drained a little too well, leaching nutrients out of top soil and often drying out under moderately hot conditions, which in Texas occurs routinely.

On one of her visits to see son Elliott, the first lady decided to visit the Gardens' "colony" and had her chauffer drive her to the project, inadvertently visiting a home not on the formal tour.

"Legend has it that the homesteader met her in his stocking feet and asked who she was," Antley wrote.

The subsistence program ended in 1936, though applications for residency continued to be accepted through the Resettlement Administration in Washington, the original one-page application slowly evolving into a torturous nine-page examination of qualifications. Still, it was a bargain, even by Depression standards. The average mortgage payment was less than $25 monthly.

The Farm Security Administration semi-officially ran the community from 1938 to 1942, a sort of self-government lapse taking place during World War II, during which residents basically looked out after themselves. In June of 1949 a majority of the "colony" residents voted to incorporate into a town, electing H.L. Rhodes as the first mayor.

In 1968 the town council changed the name from "town" to "city."

Of the five original subsistence cities, only Dalworthington Gardens remains as an autonomous community. The rest were absorbed by other municipalities. Though for many years the minimum DWG lot size was two acres, the council eventually reduced that standard to a half acre, and few of the simple four or five room homes built during the Depression survive. Dalworthington Gardens still maintains a rural atmosphere with many residents gardening, raising livestock, especially horses, and often providing stables for local FFA students. Zoning favors large lots. Dalworthington Gardens is now surrounded by Arlington and Pantego.

A census snapshot of the town in 2010 is as follows:

Dalworthington Gardens Census Demographics 2010	
Population size	2,259
Houses built since 2005	30
Owner-occupied housing	82.6%
Median household income	$63,594
Median monthly mortgage payment	$3,039
No mortgage	24.9%
Population under age 18	531
Change since 2000 in under 18	100
College degrees ages 25 and up	51.9%
Anglo	80.9%
African American	5%
Asian	7%
Hispanics and other races	7%

How did the subsistence city strategy work out? The concept began to fade in a decade or so after the community was established. In one of those quirks of supply and demand, the large lots and rural feel of the Gardens over time began to attract an affluent demographic that built large homes, often with a stable or barn for their horses. Few homes built during the Depression remain. The population today is among the most affluent in Tarrant County, as is the size of the typical mortgage payment. Most of the employed population commutes outside the Gardens, and many children residing in the city attend Arlington public schools, though a significant percentage enrolls in private schools.

New census figures underscore the uniqueness of the community of 2,259, which experienced three percent growth over the last decade. For example, the figures note that no households are listed as headed by unmarried partners, and it has some of the lowest reports of divorced people in the county.

Unemployment is virtually nonexistent (nine-tenths of one percent). Retirement income is in the top tier of most Tarrant cities. But median household income dropped by $12,000 over the past decade, much of which took place during a lengthy recession. Only one other Tarrant city showed a drop in median income, and it was less than $1,000.

The city is still mostly Anglo, but it recently opened a Vietnamese Community Center to serve a small but growing Asian community, said Waybourn.

The community has managed to maintain its rural flavor since its founding in 1936. Bogart, a former councilwoman, who organized the city's recent 75th anniversary celebration, says the community has tried to keep its country atmosphere. "It still has raccoons, roadrunners, quail, coyotes, foxes, armadillos and other wildlife roaming its acreage." she said.

"It's been fun to research the history and try to find the people and talk to them and hear their stories," she said. "People love to talk about the past, where they went to school, where their family is now, the gardens they had and the animals."

Despite being surrounded by Arlington and Pantego, Dalworthington Gardens tended to be almost enclave-like and residentially dominated for much of its existence, though that is slowly changing. Expansions of major border streets like Arkansas Lane, Pioneer Parkway, Bowen Road, and most recently Pleasant Ridge Road, have made portions of the city more attractive to commercial development, particularly at intersections like Bowen Road and Pleasant Ridge.

Chapter 7 – Education

The old saying "It's not where you start but where you finish" certainly applies to both the Arlington Independent School District and higher education entities of Arlington. AISD evolved from a handful of students in a two-story frame building that doubled as a lodge hall. Flash forward to 2011 and the district ranked as the 66th largest public school system in the nation, a district with about 8,000 employees. It is the city's largest employer and has an enrollment of almost 63,000 students.

What is now the University of Texas at Arlington began as something more akin to a prep school—very nearly failing on more than one occasion—but today the university sets a high standard for educational excellence in the thriving Dallas-Fort Worth area and beyond. Through life-enhancing research, innovative teaching, and community service, UT Arlington has branded itself literally as a Maverick whose students and faculty challenge convention and transform the world in which they live. Currently, the university's more than 33,000 students—an all-time high—study within an academic environment that offers almost 190 bachelor's, master's and doctoral degrees in an extensive range of disciplines.

Of UT Arlington's 150,000 alumni, approximately 100,000 live in North Texas. Their presence helps the university create an annual economic impact of more than $1 billion in the region, and the more than 4,000 university employees make the higher education entity one of the five largest employers in Arlington.

The third major education entity in Arlington, the Tarrant County College Southeast Campus, has a shorter history than AISD or UTA. Nevertheless, the Southeast Campus has grown from an initial enrollment of about 5,000 students two decades ago to almost 16,000 today—a growth that shows no sign of abating. It provides an affordable, quality education that offers two-year associate of science or arts degrees or a wide variety of certifications in more than 120 areas. Additionally, the campus has become a pioneer in both distance education and dual education, the latter being a way for motivated high school students to earn up to a year's worth of college credit while pursuing their diplomas.

Arlington Independent School District

Most certainly before AISD was formally created in 1902, there were other schools in Arlington, the first in the city—and probably Tarrant County—being a one-room log cabin school at Johnson Station near present-day Cooper Street and Mayfield Road. The late J.M. Houston in his memoirs recalled that back around 1878 the favorite recess play of the "big boys" at Johnson Station was practicing with six shooters. Why, even then, would students bring guns to school? It was a different era, Arlington being part of the "Wild West," and the memory of an unsuccessful but frightening Comanche attack on Johnson Station and the station school reverberated long after the Indian threat diminished.

Arlington's first proper school building was located on South Street in a two-story building. From 1878 to 1902 the faculty increased three-fold, which is to say it grew from one teacher to three. In 1902 an election was held to create an independent, tax-supported school district and it carried 201 to 84, establishing a tax rate of five cents per $100 valuation at a time when the average home price was $500. The first trustees were Thomas Spruance, J.E. Carter, B.F. Bridges, M.R Collins, L. Finger, J.H. Watson and R.W. McKnight. The school term was six months, the semester enrollment periods being adjusted for the needs of an essentially agrarian society. Parents needed their children for harvesting and other farming labor.

The original frame building was severely damaged by a windstorm in 1903, resulting in students moving to a temporary building. The district floated its first, but far from last bond issue in 1903, a $15,000, 40-year payout to finance two new school buildings, one for white students and another for African-Americans. The total assessed value of property in the district in 1903 was $764,120. The 2011 assessment was just under $21 billion and the tax rate was $1.27.2 per $100 valuation, a far distance from that original nickel tax.

Indeed, the five cent tax had increased to 22 cents per $100 valuation by 1904, providing early proof that education does not come cheaply, nor does the cost diminish. The new South Side School opened in the 1904-05 school year, the first of many new buildings to come, and H. Tarley was elected superintendent in 1907. The district originally offered 10 years of education, but in 1908 an 11th year was added and the curriculum was tweaked to meet the admission requirements of the University of Texas.

In 1909 the virtually new North Side School was destroyed by fire—soon to be rebuilt—and in 1908 the first minimum teaching credential was added, a first grade certificate. Teachers received their first pay raise, a $5 monthly bump after two years of service. Taxes, of course, went up to 30 cents. The six-month school term was changed to nine months for the 1909-10 year. And the district had its first real problem collecting taxes that year, though the numbers were not significant, $25 in 1909 and $35 in 1910. In 1913, J.A. Kooken was elected superintendent.

Kooken Educational Center

The district installed its first electric lights in 1914 and also adopted a policy of requiring teachers to have at least two years of experience. In 1920, Mrs. R.D. Covington was elected trustee, the first woman on the board and the last until Tye Christine Barnett passed voter muster 48 years later. The district's 260-student enrollment grew to 806 by 1920, and in July of 1921 the issuance of bonds of $100,000 was approved to build a new high school with a tax rate increase to pay for it, this time to 75 cents. The new building at Cooper and Abram streets served as the high school—eventually adding two new wings–until the new Arlington High School opened at Park Row and Cooper streets in 1954. For a while the original high school served as Ousley Junior High but in 1967 it was sold to UTA, where today it houses the School of Social Work.

The Depression years from 1929 through the 1930s typically showed an enrollment of about 700 in grade schools and 300 in high school. Teacher salaries were reduced during the "tight money" era. Funds were so restricted that the district asked for and received a grant from the Works Projects Administration to help build a replacement for the then-old South Side School, which burned even as application was being made to replace it. Voter's initially rejected, then approved, bonds to help support construction of the school.

In 1937, Superintendent Kooken retired, an event that really marked the end of the district's formative era.

"The public school situation in Texas during the latter part of the last century and the first part of the present century was such as to produce great irregularity in attendance and consequently many pupils were greatly retarded," Kooken wrote in his candid memoir "Thirty Friendly Years in Arlington Schools."

"Many of them withdrew from the school before they had completed the course prescribed for the elementary schools," he wrote.

"Maintaining order," Kooken said, "was a major issue."

"Under these adverse conditions the matter of discipline was a daily, if not an hourly, problem and the paddle and the strap were much in evidence every day. The same method of government was employed in the homes, and, in some cases, the new teacher became very popular with patrons because he 'knocked out' two of the bullies on the first day of the school year. Sometimes that was the best way to begin the school.

The collusion of large boys against the school executives sometimes resulted in physical combats and truancy."

But, Kooken noted, he had seen an attitudinal shift toward education during his three decades.

"This lack of cooperation began to disappear with the awakening of the general public in Texas about 25 years ago (Kooken's memoirs were published in 1941) with reference to the value of education and was the beginning of a new era in the history of education in our state."

Ben Everett replaced Kooken as superintendent and H.E. Stoker was high school principal. Stoker later was replaced as principal by W.R. Wimbish, who in 1938 became superintendent. Wimbish oversaw construction of the high school's first home economics building and first real gym, both projects being partially funded by the WPA. In 1940 Wimbish became superintendent, supervising a total district student enrollment of 1,232. In 1945 he hired a new AHS principal, James Martin, who eventually would become superintendent himself as well as a namesake for one of the district's high schools. Wimbish also insisted that the district adopt a 12-year system.

As might be expected, the World War II years put virtually a complete stop on building new school facilities. It was a brief slumber before post-war population growth would kick off an era of unprecedented expansion as Arlington evolved into one of the fastest growing cities in the nation.

Long-time Arlington Citizen-Journal Editor Charles Hawkes witnessed that growth and credited Wimbish with unifying several small schools into the Arlington system.

"Wimbish took it upon himself to consolidate a number of the smaller outlying school districts," Hawkes said in a 1975 interview. "Some pressure was exerted by a ruling that the schools here would no longer accept transfer students from the smaller elementary schools. This resulted in the consolidation of Grace Chapel, Watson, Harrison Chapel, Pantego and Johnson Station schools, greatly expanding the district."

James Martin became superintendent in 1955, initiating the rapid construction of auxiliary building to accommodate student growth, eliminating a controversial "double shift" school system. He also implemented construction of many open concept schools that were themselves controversial and which were later converted to more conventional school buildings. Martin also insisted on a junior high buffer system between elementary and high school. During much of the 1950s, '60s and '70s it was not uncommon for the district to add 1,000 students a year and to hire 50 new teachers. The number of elementary, junior high and high school locations boomed, as did the number of employees and tax rates.

Martin also oversaw the end of Arlington's segregated school system in 1965, which took place without the rancor demonstrated in so many communities. Until then, African American students attended their own AISD schools through elementary and junior high and high school students were bused 13 miles to Terrell High School in Fort Worth.

The district had grown to six high schools—the original Arlington High, along with Sam Houston, Lamar, Bowie, Martin and the newest high school, Seguin. Growth would not essentially slow until Arlington began to approach build out in the 1990s. There would be more challenges to come, for example, a voters' rejection of a higher tax ceiling in the 1990s. Also, the revamping of funding mechanisms by the state legislature has resulted in recurring financial issues that have yet to be resolved.

That tiny school district created in 1902 is now the ninth largest district in Texas. Twenty percent of the student body is enrolled in a gifted and talented program and twenty-one percent of the student body is enrolled in career or technical education programs. AISD currently offers the International Baccalaureate World School Program at Arlington, Bowie, Lamar and Sam Houston high schools. AISD plans to offer the program in all high schools in the future. The district had changes in its minority-majority demographics by the late 1990s.

AISD students have the opportunity to graduate with 30 or more college credits through the district's advanced placement program, equivalent to one full year of college study. The Advanced Placement curricula included English, calculus, biology, geography, world history, American history, American government, European history, macroeconomics, psychology, statistics, computer science, physics, chemistry, environmental science, music theory, art, art history and foreign languages.

AISD and Tarrant County College joined forces in June of 2007 to offer dual-credit choices at each high school. The district covers tuition cost and books for students who take advantage of this on-site opportunity. This partnership expanded the district's dual-credit initiative with TCC, which required students to attend courses at a TCC campus. The program was the first of its kind in this area and now serves as a state and national model.

AISD and Texas Christian University recently teamed up to strengthen the area's future nursing professionals. Qualifying AISD students are now guaranteed admission status to TCU and the Harris College of Nursing and Health Sciences. AISD is home to an award-winning and acclaimed special education program that focuses on academic success as well as the development of life skills.

For the 2010-2011 school year the budget was $438.6 million, with 49 percent coming from property taxes. The average teacher salary was about $57,000; a little more than $45,000 for a beginner, and the average years of teaching experience was 8.4. The district's administrative cost ratio was 4.18 percent, compared to the state standard of 11.05 percent for a district of comparable size. In addition to six high schools (nine if Turning Point High School, Venture High School and Newcomer Center are counted), the district has 13 junior highs and 52 elementary schools.

University of Texas at Arlington

In some ways, Arlington's early residents were more concerned about establishing higher education than they were about creating a public school system. The predecessor to UTA came into being in 1895, seven years before voters approved the Arlington Independent School District in 1902.

Edward Emmett Rankin, eventually to be considered the father of Arlington College, fostered the idea of a private preparatory school in the spring of 1895 as an option to public schools. Two of the city's leading citizens, William Trimble and Lee Hammond, endorsed the idea and— with wide community support—opened Arlington College on a block of land donated by the city in an area now occupied by the E.H. Hereford Student Center. Community members passed the hat, with Trimble and Hammond each contributing $500, also selling fifteen $100 scholarships at Rankin's suggestion. More than $5,000 was eventually collected and a two-story frame structure was erected with four classrooms on the ground floor and two classrooms, plus an assembly room upstairs. The building, with ongoing modifications, was used until the 1930s.

Though a dollar in 1895 went considerably further than today's inflated version, the price was a bargain, even at the time. Hammond, in a 1958 interview, said that the project was achieved on such a low budget through community collaboration that went beyond cash donations. Lumberyard owner Thomas Spruance sold the lumber at cost. Brickyard owner W.C. Weeks contributed some materials and sold the rest at his cost. Rankin owned a hardware store and provided materials from it at cost.

"It was," Hammond said, "a fine example of civic attitude." When bids were received for construction of the original building, an out-of-town contractor presented the lowest bid. Spruance and other residents took up a collection and paid the contractor to withdraw his bid so the contract could be given to Arlington builder C.F. Thomas.

"It was felt at the time this arrangement would be more conducive to better local support for the new school," Hammond recalled.

"The college opened in 1895 with a staff of six teachers and between 75 and 100 pupils," UTA historian Clarence Denman noted in a 1972 Citizen-Journal article. "Hammond, Trimble and H.L. Graham, an elementary grade teacher, all drew their salaries from the tuition, which ranged from $1.50 to $3.50 a month, depending on grade."

Denman said the tuition and the $1,500 from the 15 scholarships translated to a modest salary of about $360 annually for the three teachers, who were also aided by three special teachers—Molly McDonald (art), Sally Hayter (music) and Frue Lanier, an elocution instructor. The latter three were paid with separate fees.

"Because the present-day school system is so different from that of 1895, it is difficult to classify what grades were taught, but in that year (1895) elementary through high school grades can best describe the system," Denman said. "There was a great deal of overlap in the high school into college level work—much more than exists today."

In 1896-97 Arlington College began conducting an all-grades school that was free five months for students entitled to attend public schools, but tuition was charged for others during those five months and for all pupils during the remaining four months.

Since many Arlington residents did not want to close their public schools (South Street School, Johnson Station, Pantego and others), Hammond and the principal of the South Street School, W.W. Witt, called on area parents in a poll to determine which school they preferred. Most wanted their children enrolled at the college, and public funds were divided between the two—not a good situation for either entity. Though enrollment at Arlington College increased through 1898, it began to dip after that, with Trimble eventually selling his interest in the school to W.M. Glass. Both Hammond and Glass were forced to sell their interest in 1900 to citizens who formed the Arlington College Corporation.

"With enrollment less than 100, the college was rented out in 1901 to the public schools," Denman said, "but the college idea was far from dead. In 1902 the Arlington College Corporation, with M.H. Cravens as acting president, deeded the college property to three trustees: W.M. Dugan, James Ditto and J.H. Watson. Those men agreed to turn their property over to the Carlisle School if a school was operated in the building for four years."

And so it was. Carlisle Military Academy took over the building in 1902 and Arlington College Corp. ceased existence. The Carlisle School for Boys opened in 1902, the same year the Arlington Independent School District was approved by voters.

Denman said the change was the beginning of a long series of names for the institution that would eventually become the University of Texas at Arlington.

"Arlington College became The Carlisle School, which would become Arlington Training School, Arlington Military Academy, Grubbs Vocational College, North Texas Agricultural College, Arlington State College and eventually the University of Texas at Arlington," he said.

The movement to establish a branch of the Texas A&M College at Arlington began in 1907, but it was not until 10 years later that the bill was finally passed by the state legislature to make it happen.

"Oddly enough," Denman said, "the suggestion was first made in an editorial in the Houston Post in 1907." The editorial pointed out the advantages of locating a mechanical branch midway between Dallas and Fort Worth to accommodate hundreds of students who could board at home and receive their technical instruction at the school.

The initiative from that idea almost—but not quite—resulted in a decision to move Texas A&M from its College Station site to Arlington. At the time, A&M only had a capacity of about 500 students and the location between Fort Worth and Dallas was considered to have considerably more potential.

The eventual decision was for A&M to remain at College Station, but with the Arlington campus as an affiliate. On March 2, 1917, with the help of industrial education advocate Judge V.W. Grubbs of Greenville, a bill was passed in the legislature and Grubbs Vocational College was established in Arlington as a branch of Texas A&M. Grubbs—who clearly expected to be named president of the new school but was not—worked with an Arlington delegation to Austin that included Webb Rose, W.C. Weeks, Frank McKnight, J.I. Carter, Leslie Coulter and Jack Slaughter—many of whom had been involved with creation of the original Arlington College and who spent more than two decades trying to stabilize a local higher education presence.

The Arlington Journal in its April 6, 1917, edition predicted the new Grubbs Vocational College would "become the largest co-educational primary industrial school in the entire Southwest."

Growth would come, but slowly, particularly during the Depression. Grubbs, by then called North Texas Agricultural College, began a post-WWII boom that was further stimulated by yet another change of name to Arlington State College. Years later, on May 5, 1959, the college was elevated from junior college to four-year senior college status. It was a process that evolved, sometimes with considerable rancor, over more than two decades.

"What led to that change was the hardest-fought struggle the university ever faced," Citizen-Journal writer Dan Van Cleve wrote in a 1972 historical piece. "The nix had come from Tarleton College, which was not a four year school either at the time and had the same desires as Arlington State College."

As early as 1936, the Arlington Civic League called for conversion of the school to a four-year program, but legislation failed. It failed again in future sessions, handicapped by the difficulties of both the Depression and World War II. Though the 1959 bill introduced in January by state Sen. Doyle Willis was early on the lawmakers' docket, events dragged on with numerous delays. But senior status was finally approved by lawmakers and made official by Gov. Price Daniel's signature on May 5. ASC became the state's 17th four-year college.

Though Arlington residents were initially happy with the change, they quickly developed a form of buyer's remorse with Texas A&M, whose president made it clear that he believed the senior status should not have been given. Nor were local residents pleased with a 1964 proposal to change ASC's name to Texas A&M University at Arlington. Dallas officials favored the A&M proposal but Tarrant County's leadership did not, a situation that grew more complex when Gov. John Connally proposed a plan that would have merged both ASC and the University of North Texas—and others—into a UT system.

In March of 1967 an Arlington delegation including then-mayor Tom Vandergriff, state Sen. Don Kennard and J. Lee Johnson III met with the UT regents to discuss moving ASC into the UT system. A&M regents promptly withdrew several long-desired graduate programs, a move that Arlington leadership perceived as only reinforcing the need to make a change. Eventually it was an amicable divorce and re-marriage. With Connally's endorsement the legislature made it official in 1967 and also renamed ASC as The University of Texas at Arlington.

There have been snags along the way, often with controversy, ranging from changing the school mascot names from the odd "Grubworms" of Grubbs Vocational to the Old South-oriented Rebels to the current Mavericks and the dropping of football in1985. Then-President Wendell Nedderman defended the no-football decision, noting both a failure of student attendance and a million-dollar sports program deficit. Though the university endured a drop in enrollment in the late 1990s and early 2000s related to the creation of UT Dallas, in general the growth in student population and in the number of academic programs has been steady. For the 2011-2012 semester, the university enrolled more than 33,000 students who had a choice of almost 190 bachelor's master's and doctoral degrees. The university has about 2,000 full and part-time faculty members within 12 colleges and schools. The university's basketball, volleyball and baseball teams have all made NCAA playoffs in recent years, and in 2012 the university joined the high profile Western Athletic Conference (WAC). Once primarily a commuter school, the percentage of public college students living on campus is now one of the highest in the state.

The physical transformation on the campus has been dramatic for the past decade, building space increasing by almost 1.9 million feet including projects under construction through 2012. A 234,000-square-foot Engineering Research Building opened in June of 2011 and College Park Center, a $78 million, 6,500 seat venue that will host a mix of high profile events as well as the university's basketball and volleyball teams opened in the spring of 2012. The first commencement in the new center was for the College of Engineering in May 2012, 364 graduates and 5,700 guests were in attendance. College Park, a mixed-use development north of the College Park Center will wrap residence halls and street-level retail space around a four-story parking garage; all are slated to open in 2012 with considerable ramifications to both the university and to on-going downtown Arlington redevelopment. High-density privately funded student apartment complexes along Abram Street were are also expected to bring in more than 900 additional on-campus residents in 2012.

University of Texas at Arlington

UTA is also experiencing a dramatic increase in graduate research funding and is on track to become a Tier One university during this decade.

"UT Arlington's pioneering researchers help solve today's most complex problems and create viable products and services that strengthen our economy," UTA President Jim Spaniolo said. "Research activity continues to grow dramatically, vastly expanding our capacity to advance the human condition and make lasting imprints on the world."

Tarrant County College Southeast Campus

There's no doubt a certain amount of irony involved that Arlington State College switched from being a two-year junior college—the preferred term has since become "community college"—to four-year status in 1959 just as the golden age of community colleges dawned.

But as the only community college in Tarrant County, the change at Arlington State College no doubt created something of an educational vacuum, particularly for technical and occupational programs that often paid well but didn't require a four-year diploma. This need was soon addressed.

The first movement toward the establishment of a community college in Tarrant County occurred in the early 1960s when the Haltom-Richland Chamber of Commerce began investigating the possibility of establishing such an institution in that part of the county. At about the same time, Fort Worth Mayor Willard Barr established Town Hall, an action group open to the public through which community projects could be developed. Leading topics of conversation included the need for a convention center and a community college.

Dr. Bill Lace, Tarrant County College vice chancellor and the unofficial historian for the college, notes that junior colleges had been around for many years, but most of them tended to be rural and limited in scope.

"The mid-1960s saw the advent of the urban community colleges, as opposed to the junior college, the key difference being that the junior college is, by definition, "junior" to a senior college, offering the first two years toward the baccalaureate," Lace said. "The community college, on the other hand, is multi-dimensional, offering not only academic courses, but also technical or occupational programs and a wide variety of non-credit courses and programs."

The college was suggested as a Town Hall project by two prominent Fort Worth citizens, attorney Jenkins Garrett and Star-Telegram executive J. Lee Johnson, both of whom had served on Texas Gov. John Connally's blue-ribbon task force on higher education. They saw the gap that existed at the time and cited the need for an institution that would provide both technical training and serve as a starter for bachelor's degrees.

In June of 1963, the Fort Worth Chamber of Commerce commissioned a study by C.C.Colvert, a University of Texas faculty member considered the state's leading authority on junior colleges. Colvert studied the demographics of the county and the potential costs and stated that such a college was feasible. He raised some eyebrows by predicting that as many as 1,900 students might attend during the first semester.

The county had to meet three criteria—sufficient public school students, enough taxable property to support a community college system and an election petition signed by at least 10 percent of registered voters, at that time about 12,000 signatures.

Thus encouraged, Town Hall leaders joined forces with their counterparts in the northeast part of the county to begin the drive to establish a college. The county already met two of the three requirements — it contained enough "scholastics" (public school students) and it had enough taxable property. The third step was to get petitions signed by at least 10 percent of registered voters. At this time in Texas, one had to be a property owner to vote in an election involving the levying of ad valorem taxes. About 12,000 signatures were needed; the group got more than 24,000.

A citizens' committee was formed to pass the election. It consisted of a veritable "who's who" of Fort Worth, including the editors of the Star-Telegram and the Fort Worth Press, state Sen. Don Kennard,

Arlington Mayor Tom Vandergriff, and many others. It was chaired by oilman Larry Meeker. There was even a "Youth Committee" chaired by the student body president at Arlington Heights High School, 17-year-old Tom Schieffer, who later would become a member of the board of trustees, a state representative and ambassador to Australia.

Registration for the first semester in junior college history was completed on September 16, 1967. The final enrollment figure of 4,194 exceeded even the most optimistic prediction and was the largest opening-day enrollment of any single campus in community college history.

"The board did not at that time have a member from Arlington, and the feeling was that the first two campuses should be in Fort Worth and in the northeast," Lace recalled. "It was pointed out that Arlington already had Arlington State College and that it might be better to wait a while before locating a junior college campus there. A while turned out to be 31 years, with the Southeast Campus in Arlington opening in 1996."

A long delay in the construction of State Highway 360, which would be the major traffic artery serving the Southeast Campus, held up plans for the new facility. At last, in August of 1993, a $70 million bond election was held and passed comfortably. The lion's share of the money, $41 million, was for the construction of the Southeast Campus in Arlington.

The Southeast Campus opened for classes in the summer of 1996 with an abbreviated schedule, taught out of two portable buildings at Barnett Junior High School just north of the campus site. The first campus president was Dr. Judith Carrier, who remained the only president the campus had until her retirement in August of 2011. The campus itself opened in the fall of 1996–at least two-thirds of it did. The western third of the building was not ready for occupancy until November, just in time for the ceremony dedicating the campus. Built for a student population of about 5,000, the campus quickly exceeded enrollment expectations, resulting in periodic expansions.

Tarrant County College

The most recent Southeast Campus expansion took place in early 2011, a new 114,519-square foot Science and Academic Wing that provided classrooms for computer science, speech and laboratory sciences. It also featured additional office space for faculty as well as meeting areas for student organizations and the Student Activities Office. By 2011, the Arlington campus enrollment was approaching 15,000 and the campus—with Carrier's initiatives—had become one of the leading dual education programs in the U.S., a how-to-model for allowing enterprising high school students to begin taking college credit classes, often enabling them to enter college with sophomore classification. TCC's for-credit enrollment on all campuses combined in 2011 was about 51,000 per semester, with another 25,000 enrolled annually in non-credit courses.

"Although geologists, archeologists and other educators might disagree, I believe the true Great Divide in America is education—quality education," Carrier said as she neared retirement in 2011. "It's what our forefathers and foremothers perhaps thought but getting it to work with equality was a slow process until the upstarts, community colleges, got into the act and refused to leave."

Arlington Baptist College
When the Rev. J. Frank Norris' 1925 idea to create a Bible institute in Dallas didn't pan out, Norris—pastor of First Baptist Church in Fort

Worth—went with Plan B, creation of a Fundamentalist Baptist Institute.

"The institute offered a plan of systematic Bible study via radio and correspondence," noted Vickie Bryant, librarian and chief historian at Arlington Baptist College. "These Bible conferences were developed to provide concentrated pastoral training, encouragement, challenge and teaching in the truth of God's Word. In 1945 the Fundamental Baptist Bible Institute became the Bible Baptist Seminary."

Though Norris died in 1952, the classes continued, and in 1954 the 46-acre former site of Top O' Hill Terrace in Arlington was purchased. A horse barn was converted into classrooms and the former casino was used for office space, a cafeteria and classrooms. The site officially became Arlington Baptist Junior College in 1965, and many high school graduates who did not want to attend a secular or liberal arts college soon began to enroll at the small four-year college.

The school now offers graduate programs in theology, educational curriculum and educational leadership. The educational leadership degree was offered for the first time in January 2011 with 18 students enrolled. Total enrollment in 2011 is 250 and the college offers online education, as well as traditional classes.

And all those secret hidden rooms, the casino and escape tunnel, discussed in an earlier chapter, are public these days. The campus history, illustrated by old photographs, is documented on the school's Web site, www.abconline.edu. Also, campus historian Vickie Bryant offers narrated tours, which can be scheduled by calling her at the college.

Oakridge School

The Oakridge School is a coeducational, college preparatory school founded in 1979. The school opened in the 1979-1980 academic year with 85 students in the Handley United Methodist Church. In 1982, the school moved into the Handley Middle School Building.

The school presently enrolls students in preschool through 12th grade. Oakridge opened its Early Childhood Center at the present 36-acre

Pioneer Parkway campus in 1984 and added the Upper School in 1985. The 1986-1987 school year saw the completion of the Lower /Middle School Building and Student Activity Center.

In 1994, a new library and multipurpose activity center were constructed. The Information Center and Fine Arts buildings were constructed during the 1999-2000 school year and were fully operational for the beginning of the 2000-2001 school year. In September 2006, the school purchased 47.5 acres for future growth, and a security center was completed in October 2007.

Oakridge's first senior class of seven students graduated in May 1985, and all were accepted to a college of their choice. A program for three-year-old children in the Early Childhood Center began in September 1989. The school's first National Merit Scholar was named in September 1992, its first National Achievement Scholar was named in February 1995 and its first National Hispanic Scholar in 2002.

Chapter 8 – Arlington Historical Markers

Historical Marker

Perhaps because Arlington is so much of a new place, it's easy not to recognize that the city is actually one of the oldest communities in North Texas, and thus rich with a sense of history. There are numerous reminders—historical markers—placed here and there in the Arlington area, more than 60 overall. Here's a list of those markers with the locations and the exact wording and punctuation on the markers, regardless of grammatical or punctuation accuracy or political correctness. The year the markers were placed is noted at the end of each marker in parenthesis. Much of the following information is based on a survey by former Arlington Councilman Ron Wright. In general the locations as listed here run from north to south.

Randol Mill
Location: An eighth mile north and 100 yards west of Randol Mill Road and Precinct Line Road. The remains of the mill can be seen from the bridge upriver west of the bridge.

In 1856 Archibald F. Leonard (1816-1876) built a dam and grain mill at this site. Hiram Crowley became a partner. The mill became a community center and county voting place. During widespread abolition violence in 1860, Leonard's Mill was burned. It reopened in 1862 and operated during the Civil War. Owners after 1867 were H.B. Alverson and J.H. Wheeler. In 1876, R.A. (Bob) Randol (1850-1922) acquired

Wheeler's Mill. A water-driven turbine powered the mill, a circular saw, and a cotton gin. Randol Mill played an important role in the area economy and closed after Randol's Death. (1979)

Harrison Cemetery

Location: 8551 Meadowbrook Dr., Ft. Worth (east of Eastchase Pkwy near its intersection with Ederville Road.)

When first used, this one-acre cemetery belonged to Tarrant County pioneer D.C. Harrison. The earliest known grave is that of Mary E. Harrison (1864-71). Several early settlers used this site, including R.A. Randol (1850-1922), the operator of Randol Mill, who bought this tract in 1895 and deeded it forever as a burial ground. Graves here number about sixty and include those of the Edward Deason family, Randol's first wife Ronda (Harrison) (1859-82), his brother John C. Randol, who died in an 1894 mill accident, and Nancy Cannon Harrison (1833-83), mother of Ronda Harrison Randol. (1892)

Tomlin Cemetery Site

Location: At the west end of Tomlin Lane, Arlington (north of I-30 and west of Davis Street.)

This Cemetery was first used in the 1870s by the Wilkinsons, a pioneer family whose graves are marked by clusters of rock. Members of the Angel family are also buried here. The oldest dated gravestone is that of Virginia native Solomon Tomlin (b.1825), a horseman and farmer who migrated with his family to Texas in the 1860s. He died on July 9, 1884. His son, James Tives "Buck" Tomlin (1852-1934), a noted breeder of fine racing horses, bought the cemetery property in 1888. It has since been designated to serve the descendants of the Tomlin family. (1982)

Gibbins Cemetery and Homestead:

Location: 2200 N. Davis St., Arlington (north of I-30 on the east side of the road.)

James Gibbins (1817-1870) migrated to Texas from Arkansas in 1857. He bought land near present-day Arlington in 1863. Gibbins deeded part of the land to his son Thomas Jefferson Gibbins (1841-

1891), who enlarged the homestead. This family cemetery was first used for the burial of Thomas' first wife, Amanda C. Gibbins (1846-1877). His second wife, Martha H. Gibbins (1856-1924) maintained the land for three decades after the death of her husband. The Gibbins family has contributed much to this area, including the donation of land for a public school and the *Rose-Brown-May Park in 1982.

Note: Rose-Brown-May Park provided the nucleus for today's River Legacy Parks.

Sloan-Journey Expedition of 1838
Location: At the intersection of F.M. 157 (Collins Street) and Mosier Valley Road.

In the spring of 1838, Captains Robert Sloan and Nathaniel T. Journey led a group of about 90 northeast Texas frontiersmen on a punitive expedition against the Indians who had raided their homes in present-day Fannin County. The trail led them to the vicinity of present-day Euless and Arlington, where they attacked a small Indian village, killed several Indians, and recovered a few horses. The Sloan-Journey expedition is among the first known Anglo-American activities in what is now Tarrant County that helped to open north Texas to white settlement.

Bird's Fort (no longer exists)
Location: on FM 157, 1 mile south of Calloway Cemetery Rd. on FM 157, Arlington. (adjacent to Calloway Lake, the marker is on Collins Street north of the river.)

Established in 1840 by Jonathan Bird on the Military Rd. from Red River to Austin. In its vicinity an important Indian treaty, marking the line between the Indians and the white settlements, was signed September 29, 1843, by Edward H. Tarrant and George W. Terrell, representing the Republic of Texas. The ragged remnant of the ill-fated Snively expedition sought refuge here, August 6, 1843. (1936)

In an effort to attract settlers to the region and to provide protection from Indian raids, Gen. Edward H. Tarrant of the Republic of Texas Militia authorized Jonathan Bird to establish a settlement and military post in the area. Bird's Fort, built near a crescent-shaped lake one mile east in 1841, was the first attempt at Anglo-American colonization in present Tarrant County. The settlers, from the Red River area, suffered from hunger and Indian problems and soon returned home or joined other settlements. In August 1843, troops of the Jacob Snively Expedition disbanded at the abandoned fort, which consisted of a few log structures. Organized to capture Mexican gold wagons on the Santa Fe Trail in retaliation for raids in San Antonio, the outfit was disarmed by United States forces. About the same time, negotiations began at the fort between Republic of Texas officials Gen.Tarrant and Gen. George W. Terrell and the leaders of nine Indian tribes. The meetings ended on September 29, 1843, with the signing of the Bird's Fort Treaty. Terms of the agreement called for an end to existing conflicts and the establishment of a line separating Indian lands from territory open for colonization. (1980)

Note: Some evidence exists that indicates treaty discussions and signing took place at Marrow Bone Springs, located in mid-Arlington at Marrow Bone Spring Park just south of Arkansas Lane and east of Matlock Road.

Hitch Cemetery
Location: ¼ mile south of SH 183 and ¼ mile west of the county line at the dead end of Kings Port Rd., 1/10 mile east of Cambridge Rd., Ft. Worth.

This cemetery was once part of a large farm owned by Kentucky native William Henry Hitch (1818-1893), who brought his family here from Tennessee in 1855. The oldest grave in the cemetery is that of Haden T. Hitch (1846-1858), son of William H. and Esther Hitch. Besides the graves of Hitch family members, the graveyard also contains the burials of relatives in the Trigg, Liggett, and Martin families, all of whom had moved to Texas at the urging of William H. Hitch. The Hitch Cemetery stands as a visible reminder of those early pioneers. Texas Sesquicentennial 1836-1986

Jesse Chisholm's Historical Marker
Location: On the east side of S.H. 360 on the access road south of Texas

183, approximately 50 feet north of FAA Boulevard.

Founder of world-famous cattle trail Jesse Chisholm (1806-1868): Represented the Republic of Texas and President Sam Houston in many negotiations with Indians. Half Scotsman, half Cherokee, a scout, hunter, trader and trailblazer. Spoke 40 Indian languages and dialects and was a respected influence among Southwestern tribes, including the wild Kiowas and Comanches.

In 1843, near here at Bird's Fort on the Trinity, was interpreter for a peace conference; in 1849 was in negotiations for Grapevine Springs, to the north.

He is best known for marking the Chisholm Trail across Oklahoma and Kansas. Cowboys driving cattle north to seek favorable markets used his direct route, which avoided deep rivers and lay in grassy, watered land. He thus helped rebuild a Texas economy that had been wrecked in 1861-1865 by Civil War. Cattle had increased greatly in wartime. Texas had no market, drives were necessary, so $5 longhorns could go to northern markets to bring $30 or more per head. In 1867 the Chisholm Trail was extended to Abilene, Kansas, where cattle loading pens and railroad shipping cars were provided.

This was the best known of several cattle trails from Texas over which some 10,000,000 beeves were driven from the state during the years 1866-1884. (1967)

Ford Cemetery
Location: East of 602 Fountain Parkway, Grand Prairie (between and at the back of two warehouses.)

Pinkney Harold Ford (1831-1901) was the leader of a Kentucky family who migrated to Texas in 1855. They settled in the area of North Arlington, then known as the Watson Community. John J. Goodwin held the original patent to this cemetery property. The oldest marked grave is that of Maria Trayler (b. 1799), who died in 1858. Ford, a Civil War veteran, purchased this property in 1879 and designated this site as a community burial ground. He and wife Elizabeth (d.1898) farmed land nearby. Industrial development has surrounded this remnant of the pioneer community. (1982)

Note: The cemetery is located in the Great Southwest Industrial District.

West Fork United Presbyterian Church
Location: In the Great Southwest Industrial District at 905 Santerre Drive.

West Fork United Presbyterian Church: In 1870 the Rev. Andrew Shannon Hayter organized the Good Hope Cumberland Sabbath School to serve the surrounding area. The first church building, which was also used as a school house, was located in the vicinity of the Watson Cemetery (2 mi. SW) on property donated by P.A. Watson. In 1872 the congregation adopted the name West Fork. The church's third sanctuary, built two years after a destructive 1924 fire, was moved to this location in 1955 during construction of the Dallas-Fort Worth Turnpike. (1982)

P.A. Watson Cemetery
Location: 1024 N. Watson Road, SH 360, Arlington. (the northbound Texas 360 access road.)

Mrs. Micajah Goodwin was buried here in 1846, soon after her family came to this area. They constructed a coffin from their wagon bed and burned brush atop the grave to hide it from Indians. When Patrick Alfred Watson (1810-1894) of North Carolina bought the land in 1853, he set aside a one-acre cemetery. In 1870 Watson gave land and a structure was built for Watson Community's first school and church, later West Fork Presbyterian Church. In 1956 Dallas-Fort Worth Turnpike was routed around the cemetery and the church was relocated. (1979)

Six Flags Over Texas
Location: At the entrance to Six Flags Over Texas Amusement Park behind the ticket counters.

The Six Flags Over Texas: Flags of six different countries have been raised over Texas. In 1519 the land was claimed for Spain, whose explorers came later in search of silver and gold but found buffalos, Indians and mirages. They planted the red and gold banner of Spain with its lions and castles. Beside the cross of the missionaries, intent on converting the Red men, the gold and white standard of France arrived in 1658 with the expedition of La Salle.

The first resident governor of Texas, around a fort built near the Lavaca River, La Salle tried to establish a permanent colony for the king. He failed and in 1687 was killed by his own men.

French activity in Texas caused Spain to renew her interest. Finding the port of La Salle in ruins, the Spaniards in 1689 began to build missions and presidios and grant land for ranches and colonies. Smoldering rebellion in 1821 brought an end to Spanish rule. Afterward, the green, white and red flag of Mexico, with its eagles, serpents and cactus, flew in Texas for 15 years. The settlers joined together in building towns, farming and fighting Indians. Then the policies of dictator Santa Anna provoked revolution. On March 2, 1836, the Texas Declaration of Independence was adopted and signed at Washington-on-the-Brazos.

The Republic of Texas was born in the dark era of the fall of the Alamo, Goliad Massacre and "Runaway Scrape" of settlers fleeing before the coming of Santa Anna and his army. The glorious victory of the Texans at San Jacinto on April 2, 1836, established the sovereignty of the Lone Star Flag. As a nation, Texas built towns and mills; developed strong commerce; fought against the Indians and foreign raiders; established patterns of justice, with Homestead Acts and other laws; and won the respect of all the world. However, after nine years as a Republic, the people voted in favor of annexation to the United States.

On February 16, 1846, the Lone Star banner became a state flag and Texas took her position as the 28th star in the United States flag. Until 1861 no other state adopted a flag, but the Lone Star has been the pride of Texas through all the years since 1836. For 4 years, 1861-1865, the stars and bars of the Confederate States of America flew over Texas.

90,000 Texans served the South.

The state supplied large amounts of cotton, food and other goods. At the end of the Civil War, Old Glory with its stars and stripes again was raised. Some other flags have flown somewhat briefly over parts of Texas, but the six national banners shown here are those of enduring history. The exhibits associated with the Six Flags Over Texas make vivid the colorful history of the Lone Star State.

Cable Tool Rig Marker
Location: In Six Flags Over Texas Amusement Park at the entrance to the Boom Town.

Drilled the early deep oil wells in Texas. Derrick here is exact replica and has same rigging and tools used in 1920 to drill the Crowley No. 1, a 250-barrel producer at 3,500 feet—one of the deepest wells at the time. It was near Breckenridge in one of great fields in oil empires of Texas. (1966)

Hand-carved Carousel
Location: At Six Flags Over Texas Amusement Park, 2201 Road to Six Flags, opposite the main entry.

Made popular in Texas by traveling shows and carnivals. Arrival of a horse-drawn carousel in a town was a great event. Rides to tunes of the calliope helped to celebrate town site openings, completions of railroads, promotions in boom towns. The historical designation remains but the marker has disappeared. (1966)

Narrow Gauge Railway
Location: In Six Flags Over Texas, 2201 Road to Six Flags.

Economical to build, operate and maintain, many narrow gauge railroads were running in Texas between 1853 and 1900. Some were "Tops" (for towns off the main line); some logging roads, going deep into woods and swamps. Hauled passengers, thousands of cattle, tons of sugar cane or other crops, and were used for general traffic. One line— Great Sweetgum, Yubadam & Hoo Hoo—operated at first as the T.M. &

C. (Two Mules and a Car). The two engines at Six Flags over Texas were built in 1887 and 1903 and rebuilt according to original specifications.

Arlington Downs Racetrack
Location: 2225 East Randol Mill Road

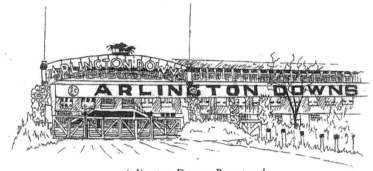

Arlington Downs Racetrack

Wealthy rancher and oilman W. T. Waggoner (1852-1934) developed a stable of fine thoroughbreds and quarter horses at his ranch here in the 1920s. At this site he built Arlington Downs, a one-and-one quarter mile race track with a 6,000-seat grandstand. Racing days drew thousands of spectators including numerous celebrities. Waggoner and his sons Guy (1883-1950) and Paul (1889-1967) campaigned for pari-mutuel betting, which was legalized in Texas from 1934 to 1937. The Racetrack was used for rodeos and other events before the buildings were razed in 1958. (1978)

Top O' Hill Terrace
Location: 3001 W. Division Street

Beulah Adams Marshall bought land here along the Bankhead Highway in the early 1920s and opened a tea room, hosting teas and serving dinners to Dallas and Fort Worth patrons.

In 1926, Fred and Mary Browning purchased the property and shortly began converting the facilities into a casino, adding an escape tunnel and secret room for hiding the gambling paraphernalia during raids.

Known as Top O' Hill Terrace, the popular spot attracted gamblers as well as visitors who were often unaware of the gaming activities. The restaurant, along with the tea garden that exists today, was a legitimate business, operating alongside a brothel as well as the casino, which benefited from the nearby Arlington Downs Racetrack.

Top O' Hill Terrace

Top O' Hill Terrace facilities included a horse barn and a private stable for Browning's prized stud, Royal Ford, purchased from oilman and Arlington Downs owner W.T. Waggoner.

First Baptist Church of Fort Worth: Contemporary to the Top O' Hill heyday was the outspoken Dr. J. Frank Norris (d. 1952), longtime pastor of First Baptist Church of Fort Worth.

The conservative Norris, co-founder of Fundamental Baptist Bible Institute, later known as Bible Baptist Seminary and later as the Arlington Baptist College, was an ardent proponent of prohibition and gambling reform.

One of his targets was Top O' Hill Terrace, which he reportedly vowed one day to own. In 1947, Texas Ranger Captain M.T. "Lone Wolf" Gonzaullas led a raid on Top O' Hill, catching the gambling operation in full swing.

In late 1956, under the leadership of Earl. K. Oldham, the Bible

Baptist Seminary bought the property and relocated here, fulfilling Norris' promise, although neither he nor Browning (d. 1953) had lived to see it.

Today, The Arlington Baptist College continues to use the site, which retains many of its original structures and features a statue of Norris by noted sculptor Pompeo Coppini. (2010) The Arlington Baptist grounds also include two smaller historical markers, one titled "Front Gates" and another titled J. Frank Norris "The Fighting Fundamentalist." Both markers are located along the main road leading into the college.

Front Gates: These original rustic gates were designed and crafted by Southern Ornament Ironworks of Arlington. Guards stationed here either welcomed or turned away patrons after checking identities. Unwelcome guests, such as local police or Texas Rangers, were allowed access, which set off an elaborate alarm system. By the time authorities reached the casino, gambling equipment would have been whisked away. Guests either slipped out the back of the property or were found sipping tea in the Tea Garden. (Top O' Hill Terrace)

J. Frank Norris: The Fighting Fundamentalist: One of Top O' Hill Terrace's most outspoken adversaries was J. Frank Norris. He was vehemently opposed to alcohol, gambling and prostitution. At a tent meeting held in Arlington in the mid-1930s, he proclaimed "Top O' Hill Terrace is a blight on Tarrant County. One of these days we are going to own the place!" His prediction came true in 1956 when Bible Baptist Seminary, now Arlington Baptist College, founded by Norris, bought the property.

This bronze statue of J. Frank Norris was created by the famous sculptor Pompeo Coppini.

City of Arlington Marker
Location: 100 S. Center Street entrance

The city of Arlington developed along the juncture of two distinct ecological regions, the blackland prairie and the Eastern Cross Timbers. The west fork of the Trinity River and its area tributaries flow through the city, and one such stream, Village (Caddo) Creek, was the site of a series of Native American communities.

The 1841 Battle of Village Creek and the 1843 Bird's Fort Treaty between the Republic of Texas and the Delaware, Chickasaw, Waco, Tawakoni, Keechi, Caddo, Nadako, Ionie, Biloxi and Cherokee tribes opened the region to pioneer settlement led by Col. Middleton Tate Johnson and Patrick Watson. In 1876, the Rev. A.S. Hayter helped survey the area for a new town site and rail stop for the Texas and Pacific Railroad. Named Arlington for the Virginia home of Gen. Robert E. Lee, the town became a regional cotton distribution center. Incorporation occurred in 1884, the year after its first newspaper, "The World", was first published. At the turn of the 20th century, the city's more than 1,000 residents supported several churches and schools, including Arlington College, an institution that became the University of Texas at Arlington in 1967.

Arlington residents adopted a city manager form of government in 1949. The municipality, situated between Fort Worth and Dallas, served as an Interurban rail hub and as a stop along the Bankhead Highway. It became a statewide destination for amusements beginning in the 1920s with gambling at Top O' Hill Terrace and horseracing at W.T. Waggoner's Arlington Downs. Later attractions included Six Flags Over Texas Amusement Park, established in 1961, and the Texas Rangers Baseball team. Today, Arlington remains a viable part of one of the nation's largest metropolitan areas. (2006)

Note: If the marker were to be installed today it would certainly include the presence of the Dallas Cowboys.

Colonel Neel E. Kearby Marker

Location: Front entrance to the Arlington downtown library, 100 S. Center Street.

Colonel Neel E. Kearby was born in Wichita Falls on June 5, 1911 to Dr. John Gallatin Kearby, Jr., and Bessie Lee (Stone) Kearby. He spent much of his childhood in Mineral Wells, but later moved to Arlington, graduating from Arlington High School in 1928 and beginning college at North Texas Agricultural College (now the University of Texas at Arlington).

In 1937, Kearby received a business degree at the University of Texas at Austin and joined the U.S. Army Air Corps. He began flight training at Randolph Field in San Antonio, where he met his future wife, Virginia King Cochran. Once commissioned, Kearby completed a series of assignments and in 1942 was selected to command the 348th Fighter Group, which trained in New England prior to combat assignments in the Pacific Theater. During that time, Kearby trained his unit to effectively deploy the P-47 Thunderbolt Fighter Plane. Although the Thunderbolt was known to be bulky and cumbersome, Kearby developed aggressive tactics that his pilots used with great success against the enemy.

During a six-month period in 1943 and 1944, Kearby led missions in his P-47 (named the Fiery Ginger after his wife), accumulating 22 aerial victories, including the destruction of a then-record six enemy aircraft in a single mission on October 11, 1943. The events of that day earned Kearby the Medal of Honor, the nation's highest award for valor. His final mission occurred on March 5, 1944, after downing an enemy bomber.

During his military career, Kearby also earned two Silver Stars, four Distinguished Flying Crosses, five Air Medals and the Purple Heart. His body was recovered after the war and buried at Hillcrest Memorial Park Cemetery in Dallas on July 23, 1949. (2009)

Andrew Hayter Marker and Markers for the Collins, Ditto, Rogers, Rose, Rankin and Cooper Families
All of these markers are historically significant.

Location: Founders' Park Plaza, 100 W. Abram St., in the Downtown/University District. The seven historical markers are located in the park at the entrance to the Levitt Pavilion, southwest corner of Center and Abram streets.

Andrew Hayter: Andrew Hayter is known as one of the earliest settlers in the area, which became known as Arlington in 1876. He is considered to be the father of Arlington. A native of Tennessee, Hayter moved to Tarrant County in 1869 and became a preacher and land surveyor. A small settlement developed on the edge of Hayter's property, and he petitioned for a post office in 1875. The post office was called Hayterville.

Hayter had already founded two churches, a school and Masonic Lodge when he was asked in 1876 to help locate the railroad through the eastern, most peaceful route of Tarrant County. He was asked to lay out a half-mile square settlement between Dallas and Fort Worth.

According to historians, railroad designers relied on Hayter for timber and surveying knowledge. When the work was done, the railroad offered to name the town Hayter, but the reverend declined the offer. He gave the town the name Arlington, which was the name of General Robert E. Lee's Virginia estate. The birth of Arlington led to the demise of Hayterville, and the post office was moved to Arlington.

Collins Family: Four Collins brothers and their families migrated to the area, first leasing land on Arkansas Lane. By 1876, they had moved into the new town of Arlington.

William Joseph Collins (1830-1905) was a farmer. His farm was in the vicinity east of present day Collins Street and north of Division Street. He was often referred to as "Uncle Joe" and was keenly interested in schools and education.

Rice Woods Collins (1838-1912) was a merchant. He opened the R.W. Collins and Co., a mercantile establishment located at the southwest corner of Center and Main Streets. As the need for a public well in the center of town became evident, R.W. took the lead in soliciting subscriptions for the cost of drilling. Unfortunately, the water was not drinkable because of the high mineral content. He was also a stockholder in Arlington College (UTA). His daughter, Mittie, was the first baby girl born in the new town.

Thomas B. Collins served for a time as County Treasurer and was Mayor of the City of Arlington from 1902 until 1904. Among the items discussed during his term were a curfew law and an ordinance regulating the boarding of interurban electric cars within the city limits.

Marshall Collins was in the real estate business. He also served as a school trustee for Arlington Independent School District after it was established in 1905. Arch Woods Collins (A.W.), son of William, played a significant role in expanding the Arlington Light and Power Company, overseeing the installation of a system of water works all over the city. He was also one of several citizens who gave land for Arlington College in 1895. He continued to support Carlisle Military Academy in 1905 and Arlington Training School in 1913. In March, 1909, Dr. Joseph Donald Collins, also son of William, had the water from the mineral well analyzed and decided to build a sanitarium on South Center Street near Border Street with the water used for treatment of patients.

Third generation Benton Carter Collins, descendant of Thomas B., served several years as City Secretary and is sometimes given credit for the naming of Collins Street. The Collins Brothers left lasting impact and a long line of descendants.

Cooper Family: James Daniel Cooper (1841-1913) moved to Arlington in 1875 and settled on a several hundred acre farm. In 1878, he built a home for his family about four miles outside the western city limit. Five sons, James Newton, William, John, Oscar and Horace were raised on the home place.

Mr. Cooper was one of the thirteen men who met at Shultz Lumber Company in 1878 to form the Centenary Methodist Episcopal Church, South (First United Methodist Church). His name is on the cornerstone. He was also an early contributor of land and money to build Arlington College, forerunner of The University of Texas at Arlington.

In the early 1920's,(sic) Cooper Street, once a pasture shortcut through the Cooper property, was named in his honor. By this time the property was within the city limits of Arlington.

His son, James Newton Cooper, built the Cooper Hotel in 1928. This historic building still stands on the northwest corner of Division and Center Streets. Two of James Newton's children, Mary and Howard, were life-long resident of Arlington. Son Horace retained ownership of the original family home until 1953 when the property was sold to UTA. The home was given to the City and was relocated to a site near Meadowbrook Park on Willis Street for use as a library. When a larger library was needed by the City, the home was rented to the Arlington Woman's Club for use as a meeting place. The women cared for it until it was destroyed by a vandal-set fire on Halloween 1998.

The house was designated a Texas Historical Landmark in 1965.

Ditto Family: Michael Ditto was one of the earliest settlers and the first of the Ditto family to arrive from Madison County, Alabama. He located to the northeast part of present-day Arlington, even before the railroad arrived or the town site was laid out.

At age eighteen, Webster Ditto, Michael's grandson (1850-1931), soon followed. After his arrival, Webster urged his father, James Ditto, Sr., (1823-1901) to join him. Webster eventually owned and farmed thirty acres, located between present day Fielder Road and Davis Drive. Later, he would do much of the post office work in the new town of Arlington.

James Ditto followed his father and son to Arlington in 1873 as a widower, bringing children, Sarah "Sallie" and John with him. Married daughter Cordelia "Delia" and husband J.P. Rose joined them. James's wife Elizabeth died prior to their leaving Alabama. James and Webster opened a general store in what is now the northeast part of present-day Arlington, in Rev. Hayter's settlement. When the town site of Arlington was platted, James Ditto, or Uncle Jimmy, as he was known, decided to move his business to the new town. He built his new store, the first in Arlington, in the middle of the block on the west side of Center Street, half a block south of Main Street.

James became Arlington's first Postmaster in 1877, with the post office located in his store. He is one of the persons given credit for naming the town of Arlington. He and his family were members of the Centenary Methodist Episcopal Church, South.

In 1895, James Ditto gave land for the founding of Arlington College, forerunner of the University of Texas at Arlington, to help bring a better source of education to the town's children. The College served students from grade one through ten.

Rankin Family: Edward Emmett Rankin (1840-1911) and his wife Edna Jerusha Broiles Rankin were encouraged to move to Arlington in 1874 by Dr. Stokley Broiles. They had six children: Rebecca, Wilson, Emmett, Edward, Wallace and Sue. They farmed on Arkansas Lane for eight years and then moved to town. Edward opened the Rankin Hardware Company which sold almost anything you could name. It was located in the 100 block of East Main Street and operated until it had to close because of the Great Depression.

By the late 1890s, daughter Rebecca had received her teaching degree and was teaching in Arlington's under-funded and poorly equipped public school system. In 1895, Emmett Rankin encouraged others to join him in establishing Arlington College, a private school for students in grades one through ten. Over the years, the College evolved into the present day University of Texas at Arlington.

The Rankins were very civic minded and Emmett's contributions included becoming the first Justice of the Peace in 1885, serving as a Director of Citizen's National Bank, and serving as Mayor from March 10, 1885 until April 10 the same year. Because of this he was often called "Squire" Rankin. He also was instrumental in securing land for the building of the Christian Church (First Christian Church) at the corner of Mesquite and South Streets in 1893.

Third generation Arlington residents included grandchildren Edward III, Robert, Edna and Bess. Edward E. and Edna graduated from Arlington Training School, (1913-1916) the third incarnation of Arlington College. Bess taught in the Arlington Public Schools for thirty years, and Bess Rankin Elementary School is named in her honor.

Rogers Family: Caroline "Carrie" Coleman Rogers (1861-1947) spent her fifteenth birthday, (July 19, 1876) celebrating the first train to stop at what would become Arlington. Between 1876 and 1880, Reverend Lewis King, Carrie's maternal grandfather, opened a small store, built a hotel on Main Street and moved the family permanently into town from nearby farmland. Carrie, involved in the daily operations of the family business, acquired skills that served her well throughout her life. In 1877 the family became charter members of the Methodist Episcopal Church, South.

Andrew Jackson "A.J." Rogers (1860-1919) came to Arlington in 1881, establishing the A.J. Rogers Dry Goods Company by 1882, located on Main Street close to the King Hotel. A.J. and Carrie married March 27, 1883 and were blessed with five children. The couple eventually owned the largest chain of dry goods stores west of the Mississippi River, as well as, the Rogers Brick factory and interests in Arlington Cotton Oil Company, a cattle ranch and an oil well. Their successful business ventures enabled the couple to become deeply involved in building Arlington socially, culturally and philanthropically.

The couple built a seven and one half acre estate that included a barn, pasture land, several orchards, large vegetable gardens, large and extensive flower gardens, a green or hot house, a stock pond, Arlington's first swimming pool built in 1892, and a structure in the front yard known as the "Owl's Nest"—a dramatic spiral staircase ascending into a tree house. The grounds of the estate were the site of many lavish social functions for the entire town, as well as annual hosting of Juneteenth celebrations.

A.J. served as the first city secretary of the Town Council in 1884, as trustee, purchased the first stock certificates in Arlington College in 1895. By 1900 he was president of the Board of Directors of the College.

Carrie served her church, volunteered at the Berachah Industrial Home for the Redemption of Erring Girls, began the Ladies Aid Society, the Cemetery Society, the first Arbor Day, the Social and Dramatic Club, the Improvement Society, the Civic League, a "Flower Ministry," wrote many articles for the Journal and other newspapers, and tirelessly urged the Town Council to focus on the betterment of the community.

After her divorce in 1902, Carrie remained in Arlington, retaining title to all the real estate the couple owned in Arlington. She continued to be a civic and business leader, especially in real estate, building rent houses and a second hotel. In 1914 she became the first woman City Marshall, later renamed Chief of Police, the first woman in the state of Texas to achieve that office in a time when women could not vote. Another first for the woman who was the "first woman" in so many other things.

Rose Family: James Preston Rose and his wife Cordelia "Delia" Ditto Rose, the daughter of James and Elizabeth Ditto, migrated from Guntersville, Alabama to Greenwood, Mississippi where they lived for several years prior to moving to Arlington, Texas in 1876. The family home was on the northeast corner of Abram and Mesquite Streets, not far from Centenary Methodist Episcopal Church, South (First United Methodist Church), where they were charter members.

William H. Rose, born in Arlington in 1883, was the son of James and Delia Rose. He married Ollie Gibbins, daughter of pioneer James Gibbins, who moved to what is now north Arlington in 1860. Ollie was born in Arlington in 1884, the same year that Arlington was incorporated. They were also members of Centenary Methodist Episcopal Church, South (First United Methodist Church).

William was a merchant, real estate developer and Mayor of Arlington from 1919-1923. His vision for Arlington was great. During his administration, Arlington's first City Charter was adopted in 1920, city audits were initiated, a variety of ordinances were passed, the first sidewalks were laid, a modern water system was established and new businesses were formed.

Education was of utmost importance as evidenced by the sale of bonds for the building of Arlington's first high school on Cooper Street.

In 1908, he and R.A. Mitchell were partners in the Rose & Mitchell real estate business. William and his brother Web owned and operated the Rose Brothers Realty Company. Among other areas in Arlington, William developed the 500-600 blocks of South Center Street, which as known as the South Center Street Historic District, listed on the National Register of Historic Place in 2003. He resided with his wife Ollie Gibbins Rose and daughters Berta and Margaret Leslie in the first home constructed within this district.

P.A. Watson Log House
Location: Knapp Heritage Park, 201 W. Front Street

After his wife Margaret Ann (Armstrong) died, Patrick Alfred Watson (1810-1894) built this dwelling in 1855 near present Arlington for their six children. In 1858 he married Margaret's niece Mary Jane Donaldson and they had six children. A surveyor, educator, and religious leader, Watson gave land for the P.A. Watson Community Cemetery and for the original site of a church and school building. The congregation is now West Fork United Presbyterian Church in Grand Prairie. The house was enlarged and Watson family descendants occupied it until 1961. *It was moved here in 1976.

Note: The house was originally moved to the Johnson Plantation Cemetery and then to Knapp Heritage Park.

Jopling-Melear Log Cabin
Location: Knapp Heritage Park, 201 W. Front Street

George Washington Jopling (1833-1903) erected this log cabin in 1863 in the Johnson Station Community for his wife Catherine (Thomas) (1837-1882) and their large family. A farmer, cattleman, and cotton gin owner, Jopling also served as a community leader, helping organizing the Johnson Station Masonic Lodge. After Catherine died he remarried and deeded the cabin, which had been enlarged, to his daughter Jane Catherine (1854-1940) and her husband Z.T. Melear (1850-1931). Melear, a farmer and blacksmith, owned a livery stable and cotton gin

Note: The cabin was originally moved to the Johnson Plantation Cemetery and then to Knapp Heritage Park. In 1970 the cabin was moved to this site. (1980)

North Side School
Location: Knapp Heritage Park, 201 W. Front Street

North Side School: After Arlington's North Side School at 433 North Center burned in 1909, this board and batten structure was built on the school grounds. Two grades met here for one term until a new brick building was erected. Contractor Joseph Crawley, who built this structure, bought it and moved it to 304 South Pecan. It served as his office until 1924 when it became a storage shed

Note: In 1977 Arlington's oldest existing schoolhouse was relocated here. The school was originally moved to the Johnson Plantation Cemetery and then to Knapp Heritage Park.

John A. Kooken Elementary School
Location: 423 N. Center Street

Arlington's North Side School opened in 1907 at the corner of Sanford and Center streets. Grades one through seven attended the new school. The building was destroyed by fire in 1909. While the school was being rebuilt, students temporarily met in a building on the property and later in a cottage.

In 1938, school officials sought Works Progress Administration (WPA) funding in building a new school, which opened in 1939. The old building was torn down and material salvaged for other structures. Housing grades one through eight, the school was renamed in honor of educator John A Kooken (December 17, 1863—May 14, 1943), who came to Arlington from Ferris (Ellis Co.) in 1908 and became the high school principal. He was elected superintendent of public schools in 1913 and served in that capacity until 1937. Kooken was known for his understanding and patience with students. In 1941, he published a memoir about his years as an educator.

Kooken Educational Center

In the early 1950s, additional wings were added to the facility. In 1976, the school closed and was used as a diagnostic and materials center before reopening in 1988 as the only preschool campus in the district. Known today as Kooken Education Center, the facility has been honored for work in integrating preschoolers with disabilities with the general student population. Today, over 100 years after North Side School was established, the institution's legacy lies in the generations of students who learned at the school and in being renamed after one of the most important educators in Arlington's history. (2010)

Carver Dixon King
Location: 301 E North Street

Carver Dixon King: Born on May 18, 1843 in Tennessee, C.D. "Uncle Dutch" King was an early leader in Arlington. He moved to Texas in 1873 and became Arlington's first Mayor shortly after the town was established in 1876; he again served as Mayor from 1899-1900.

King also worked as a notary, owned a grocery store and icehouse, and served 13 terms as Justice of the Peace. He was devoted to the community, serving on city boards and organizations when not in office.

King had two children with his first wife, Reola Eunice (Buford). After her death, he married Ione Fort. C. D. King died in 1930 and was interred in Parkdale Cemetery; today, he is remembered as one of Arlington's earliest and most dedicated leaders. (2010)

First Baptist Church of Arlington
Location: 300 S. Center Street.

First Baptist Church

First Baptist Church of Arlington: In the 1870s this church was organized at Johnson Station, an early Tarrant County settlement and stagecoach stop. In 1876 the Texas and Pacific Railroad built a line through the area and founded Arlington.

The church and other institutions moved to the new town. Worship services were held at several meeting sites before the congregation built a sanctuary at Pecan and Abram streets in 1917. That church building burned in 1944, and an auditorium was constructed on South Center Street in 1947. A new sanctuary at this location was added in 1959. (1982)

First United Methodist Church of Arlington
Location: 313 N. Center Street.

This congregation was established soon after the Texas and Pacific Railroad line was laid through Arlington. In 1877 the Rev. J.T.L. Annis was appointed pastor of the Arlington circuit, which served several area communities, including Arlington. Some of the fellowship's early worship services were held at Schultz's Lumber Yard on Front Street.

Methodist Church

By 1900, however, a small frame church building had been erected at this site, and Sunday schools, mission activities, and a women's division had been organized. Church membership continued to grow over the years, and facilities were added and expanded to meet the need.

Known as Centenary Methodist Episcopal Church, South, until 1948, the congregation then was called First Methodist Church of Arlington until 1968, when the current name was adopted. First United Methodist Church of Arlington historically has been a strong supporter of youth programs, the business and professional communities, the elderly, and education. Numerous Arlington schools have been named for members of this congregation who have provided significant service to community education. (1984)

Hutcheson-Smith Home
Location: 312 N. Oak Street.

Built about 1896, this residence reflects influences of the Queen Anne style, including gingerbread trim. It is located on land owned in the 1890s by I.L. Hutcheson, a pioneer merchant of the Arlington area, and his son William Thomas Hutcheson, who later became an oilman in Archer City.

In 1919 the house was purchased by S.T. Smith, a former educator and farmer. Owned by his family until the late 1970s, it serves as a reminder of Arlington's early development. (1982)

J.D. Cooper House
Located at the entrance to Meadowbrook Park, 211 Willis St., Arlington. (a fire caused by a Halloween prankster destroyed the home.)

Cooper House

The J. D. Cooper House was built 1878 by J.D. Cooper, an early landowner. Colonial design with square nails, wide board floors. Moved here by city. (1965) For many years the house functioned as the city library and also as home to the Arlington Woman's Club.

Fielder House
Location: 1616 W. Abram Street.

Local landowner and community leader James Park Fielder (d. 1948) and his wife Mattie (Barnes) (d. 1950) erected this house in 1914, using steel lathing and other innovative techniques. The brick Prairie style structure had a large basement to provide storage space for the fruits and vegetables grown on surrounding acreage.

Fielder House

Known as "The Home on the Hill," the Fielder residence was a popular gathering place and a landmark for citizens of Arlington. (1979)

The University of Texas at Arlington
Location: The historical marker is located in front of the university's central library, next to the flagpoles.

Tracing its history to a series of private schools and military academies, The University of Texas at Arlington has grown with the community to become one of the area's most important public institutions.

Arlington College, a private school for students in grade 1-10, opened here in 1895 in a two-story frame building. It was succeeded in 1902 by Carlisle Military Academy, operated by former State Superintendent of Public Instruction James M. Carlisle. Financial difficulties forced the Academy into receivership, and in 1913 H.K. Taylor opened Arlington Training School in its place. It in turn was replaced in 1916 by Arlington Military Academy, which closed after only one year. The school became a state-supported institution in 1917. Known as Grubbs Vocational College for local supporter Vincent W. Grubbs, it was affiliated with Texas A&M (then called The Agricultural and Mechanical College of Texas) through two more name changes--

North Texas Agricultural College (1923-49) and Arlington State College (1949-65). Transferred to the University of Texas System in 1965, it was renamed the University of Texas at Arlington in 1967 and has become the second largest University in the System, offering undergraduate and graduate degrees. Sesquicentennial of Texas Statehood 1845-1995

Site of Berachah Home and Cemetery
Location: in Doug Russell Park, U.T.A. campus on Mitchel St., Arlington. (northwest corner of Doug Russell Park just west of Davis).

The Berachah Rescue Society was organized at Waco in 1894 by the Rev. J. T. Upchurch (b. 1870) for the protection of homeless girls and unwed mothers. Nine years later he opened the Berachah Industrial Home at this site. Ten buildings were located here, including a print shop publication of the "Purity Journal". The cemetery, which contains more than eighty graves, was first used in 1904 for the burial of Eunice Williams, one of the residents. The home closed in 1935, but the site was used until 1942 as an orphanage run by Upchurch's daughter Allie Mae and her husband Frank Wiese. (1981)

Johnson Station Cemetery
Location: 1100 W. Mayfield Road at South Cooper St., Arlington

Now a part of Arlington, this area was established in the 1840s as a ranger station and trading post known as Johnson Station. This cemetery serves as a reminder of that early settlement. The oldest marked grave in the cemetery is that of Elizabeth Robinson, who died November 15, 1863. A number of unmarked graves may date from an earlier time period. A variety of gravestone styles may be found here, marking the burial sites of pioneer settlers, veterans of the Civil War, and charter members of an early Masonic Lodge. Texas Sesquicentennial 1836-1986.

First Stagecoach Inn
Location: 1000 W. Mayfield Road.

This is the site of the first Stagecoach Inn, serving as an overnight stop between Ft. Worth and Dallas. It was placed by the Lucretta Council Cochran Chapter of the Daughters of the American Revolution 1957.

Note: This is a Daughters of the American Revolution marker, not a Texas historical marker, but is a significant point of interest. The site was also briefly the home of the father of Tarrant County, Col. Middleton Tate Johnson and also the location of an Indian attack, as well as the core of the Johnson Station community.

Marrow Bones Spring

Location: Marrow Bone Spring Park on a trail connecting Vandergriff Park and the intersection of Arkansas Lane and Matlock Road. The spring is still there.

Note: This site is also credited for the being the location of the Treaty of Bird's Fort, a claim also made by the Bird's Fort marker.

An Indian habitat in the 1700s or earlier, Marrow Bone Spring in 1843 was visited by President Sam Houston's envoys seeking peace. A trading post licensed by the Texas Republic opened in 1845 near the Spring. Hiram Blackwell of the Peters Colony pioneered here before 1848. Soldier-statesman Middleton Tate Johnson (1810-1866) posted troops nearby in the late 1840s.

The first Post Office in Tarrant County opened on Oct. 31, 1851, at Johnson's Station. In 1852 Blackwell sold Johnson his rights to land surrounding the spring. The Village of Johnson's Station flourished for many years. (1979)

Woods Chapel Baptist Church,

Location: 2424 California Lane.

On April 28, 1901, a group of worshippers gathered together in a brush arbor to organize a church congregation. Led by the Rev. Washington Lafayette Wood, a missionary who had arrived in Tarrant County from Alabama in 1891, the members immediately began the task of building a sanctuary on land donated by Sam McMurray.

A small white frame structure was dedicated at this site in November 1901 and the church was named for the Rev. Mr. Wood.

Worship services were conducted on both Saturdays and Sundays until 1910. Baptismal services were held in the nearby Rush and Village Creeks until 1912, when the congregation began to use a stock tank on the property of church member Will Moore.

In 1928 the congregation called its first full-time Pastor, the Rev. C.W. Walton. Additional property was purchased in 1937, and an educational building was erected. The Rev. Mr. Walton continued to lead the congregation through the difficult years of the Depression, serving as Pastor until his death in 1941. The church continued to grow over the years. A new sanctuary, built in 1948, is still in use as a chapel for special services

Village Creek
Location: on the 7th tee at Arlington Golf Course, Arlington. (1516 Green Oaks Boulevard.)

Archeological excavations along the course of this Trinity River tributary have unearthed evidence of several prehistoric villages. Artifacts from the area date back almost 9,000 years and represent a culture of food-gatherers and hunters.

In the 1830s the Creek served as a sanctuary for several Indian tribes who made frequent raids on frontier settlements. The conflict grew worse in 1841 when major attacks were reported in Fannin and Red River Counties. Brigadier General Edward H. Tarrant (1796-1858) of the Republic of Texas Militia led a company of volunteers in a punitive expedition against Indian villages in this area. On May 24, 1841, following brief skirmishes at several encampments, two scouting patrols were attacked near the mouth of the Creek and retreated to the main camp. Reportedly twelve Indians and one soldier, Captain John B. Denton, were killed.

As result of the Battle of Village Creek, many tribes began moving west. Others were later removed under terms of the 1843 Treaty signed at Bird's Fort (10 mi. NE) which opened the area to colonization. Much of the battle site is now located beneath the waters of Lake Arlington.

Note: Some historians contend the Battle of Village Creek took place along the creek north of current-day Lake Arlington, closer to the Trinity River.

General Edward H. Tarrant, Battle of Village Creek
Location: Spur 303 (Pioneer Parkway) West of Green Oaks Boulevard.

In this vicinity, May 24, 1841, General Edward H. Tarrant with 70 men attacked several Indian villages situated along a creek (now called Village Creek) and recovered many horses and much stolen plunder. Twelve Indians were killed and many wounded of (sic) the Texans. Captain John B. Denton was killed. Captains Henry Stout and Griffin (sic) were wounded. Erected by the State of Texas 1936.

Handley Cemetery
Location: Spur 303 (E. Rosedale Street,) Fort Worth east of Loop 820 at the Handley Power Plant.

This burial ground originally served the pioneer settlers of the Handley Community, which developed here soon after the Texas and Pacific Railroad built a line to the area in 1876. The earliest marked grave is that of Jane E. Thomas (1832-1878). A church building, constructed on adjacent land in 1882, was located here for 48 years. Several early residents are buried at this site, including Civil War veteran Maj. James M. Handley (d. 1906), for whom the town was named, were later reinterred in the nearby Rose Hill Cemetery. The last burial here was in 1967. (1981)

Handley Power Plant and Lake Erie
Location: 6604. E. Rosedale Street, Fort Worth.

The Northern Texas Traction Company built the original plant at this location to generate electrical power for the Fort Worth-Dallas Interurban. Lake Erie provided water for plant operations. The area developed as a park and became popular for local outings and social events.

A two-story auditorium extended over the edge of the lake. When interurban traffic declined the park was closed. The power plant was expanded to meet increased electrical demands. In 1956 Lake Arlington became the new source of water for the Handley Plant, and Lake Erie was drained. (1980)

Note: Arlington's first electrical power source was the Handley Power Plant. Electricity—originally direct-current instead of today's alternating current—was provided when the Interurban stopped running at night.

Fort Worth/Dallas Interurban
Location: 6604 E. Rosedale Street, Fort Worth

Fort Worth/Dallas Interurban: In 1901 the Texas Legislature authorized the Northern Texas Traction Company of Fort Worth to extend rail service to Dallas. The interurban system, powered by overhead electrical lines, was completed one year later.

Note: The thirty-five mile trip took just over an hour. Passengers could flag the train and board at any point on the route. Each car held up to forty travelers.

Rail traffic began to decline in the 1930s when paved roads were constructed between the two cities, and the last train made the interurban run on Christmas Eve, 1934. (1980)

Note: The Interurban made several stops in Arlington, its route being along Abram Street.

Tate Springs Baptist Church
Location: Intersection of Little Road and Pleasant Ridge Road.

Prior to the formation of area churches, worship services were conducted at camp meetings on Village Creek. On Feb. 5, 1882, ten local residents met to organize the Tate Springs Baptist Church. Presiding over the meeting were elders M.T. Walker and D.B. Brown. The Joplin Schoolhouse (1 mile East), located on land donated by E.C. Tate, served as the first chapel. The church moved to this site in 1895 and became the center of the rural settlement. A leader in community activities, Tate Springs Baptist Church experienced rapid growth in the 1970s as a result of nearby urban development.

Dalworthington Gardens Marker
Location: On the northwest side of the intersection of Roosevelt Drive
and California Lane in Dalworthington Gardens.

The city of Dalworthington Gardens began as a result of President
Franklin D. Roosevelt's Depression-era policies. Roosevelt supported a
"back-to-the land" movement, encouraging urban workers to live on and
cultivate rural property. Roosevelt signed the National Industrial
Recovery Act into law in 1933; it authorized the establishment of a
subsistence homestead program. While visiting the area, First Lady
Eleanor Roosevelt saw this area as a site for the homestead project.

In December 1933, a corporation was formed for a state charter and
titled Dalworthington Gardens, Inc., (combining the names of nearby
Dallas, Fort Worth and Arlington). Early the next year, the federal
government bought property south of Arkansas Lane near Arlington. By
June, civil works administration workers arrived to clear the area for 80
development sites. Only people from the Dallas or Fort Worth area
would qualify to live in Dalworthington Gardens.

By May 1935, most of the construction was complete. However,
applicants that moved into the homes had to deal with many issues,
including lack of gas, faulty water and sewage piping, and unfenced
property. Residents, however, worked together to build a tight-knit
community. They soon established a community house that became a
center of activity.

In 1949, residents petitioned to have the colony incorporated into a
town. Today, though surrounded by Arlington and Pantego,
Dalworthington Gardens remains the only subsistence homestead project
existing as an autonomous community in Texas. (2010)

Tate Cemetery
Location: 4000 block of Pleasant Ridge Road (not visible from the road).
Traveling east immediately past the Woodside intersection, walk the
gravel path up the hill.

Tate Cemetery: E.C. Tate (1832-1885) came from Georgia to settle this land about 1872. He formed the Tate Springs Community here and helped organize the Tate Springs Church in 1882. Tate was buried at this site, and by 1894 three of his children also had been laid to rest here. In that year Tate's son Robert designated the burials and one acre as the community cemetery.

Robert Tate's later grave is recorded but unmarked, as are some 35 other burials. Most graves belong to members of the Tate family and the old community. In 1965 funds were raised for a perimeter fence and entry arch.

Rodgers Cemetery
Location: ¼ mile N. of Shady Oak Dr., on Little School Rd., Kennedale – on private property. (it is not easily visible from the road, nor is its marker. The marker and an entrance to the cemetery driveway are located south of 906 Little School Road, in Kennedale.)

Georgia native Thomas F. Rodgers (1835-1906) and his wife Mary (Adams) (1842-1912) came to Texas from Kansas in the late 1850s. A successful farmer and stock raiser, Thomas Rodgers later served in the Confederate Army during the Civil War. Eventually he became one of Kennedale's leading landowners. Part of his property was later set aside for this burial ground. Although most of the interments here are for Rodgers family members, the earliest marked grave is that of L.G. Patterson (1883-84), a son of the Rodgers' early neighbors.

Snider Cemetery
Location: Snider Cemetery is located ¼ mile north and west of the intersection of Kennedale's New Hope Road the Hudson Village Creek Road in a heavily wooded area north of the creek.

Born about 1805 in South Carolina, Joe Snider (d. 1887) moved his family to Shelby County, Texas, in the early 1840s. By 1856 they had settled on this property near present-day Kennedale. This part of the land came to be used as a cemetery by Snider's family and neighbors. The oldest readable marked grave is that of Daniel McVean (1800-1858), a stonecutter from New York. Snider was a farmer, merchant, and an active Mason. He and his wife Jeanette (Hudson) (1800-1878) are both buried here. Several other citizens of the Republic of Texas are buried in this pioneer cemetery. (1982)

Gibson Cemetery
Location: at 7420 Gibson cemetery Court, Ft. Worth. (500 feet south of Gibson Cemetery Road at the end of a private driveway)

In 1853 Garrett and James Gibson, along with other family members, came to Tarrant County and established 160-acre homesteads in a settlement that came to be known as the Gibson Community. Each brother donated land at this site for use as a cemetery. The earliest marked grave is that of Garrett Gibson's infant grandson, James Truitt (d. 1866). All but two of the seventy-three marked graves, many of which have only fieldstones, are for relatives of the Gibson family. The cemetery now serves as a reminder of one of Tarrant County's earliest settlements. (1983)

Earle C. Driskell Marker
Location: 100 block of U.S. Highway 287, Mansfield. a quarter mile south of F.M. 157 (Cooper Street) south of the S.H. 496 intersection on the east side of the road.

Earle C. Driskell: Born in Indiana in 1883, Earle Claud Driskell came to Texas with his parents in 1888. Educated as a lawyer, he started his journalism career in 1907 when he joined the staff of the Fort Worth "Star." He soon gained recognition for his work as an advocate of a county bond program to improve the quality of local roads and highways. Largely through his editorial efforts, a major road bond package was passed in 1911 that set an example for other state and local highway programs. Driskell died of smallpox at his Fort Worth home the following year. Texas Sesquicentennial 1836-1986.

Cumberland Presbyterian Cemetery
Location: at Mansfield Cemetery, on Burl Ray Rd. 1/10 mile west of FM 917, Mansfield. (behind the newer section of Mansfield Cemetery.)

This site was first used as a burial ground shortly after the Civil War. The earliest legible gravestone is that of Julia Alice (Boisseau) Mann (1843-68). Her husband, Ralph S. Mann, and brother-in-law, Julian Feild, founded Mansfield (originally spelled Mansfeild). The burial site was deeded to the Mansfeild congregation of the Cumberland Presbyterian Church in 1874. Graves include those of Civil War veterans and victims of the 1918-19 influenza epidemic. The oldest section in Mansfield Cemetery, the burial ground serves as a reminder of the area's earliest settlers. (1982)

Note: Mansfield originated as the (Ralph) Mann and (Julian) Feild Mill and was called "Mansfeild" but the name evolved into "Mansfield."

Ralph Mann Homestead
Location: 604 W. Broad Street, Mansfield

A native of South Carolina who came to Texas in the 1850s, Ralph Sandiford Mann (1825-1907) was one of the founders of Mansfield. The town was named for Mann and his brother-in-law and business partner Julian Feild.

The two men operated a steam-powered grist mill that supplied grain to the Confederacy during the Civil War (1861-1865) and later to U.S. troops at Fort Belknap and Fort Griffin. Mann built the original log portion of this home for his family about 1866 and later added the brick rooms. He donated land for Mansfield Cemetery, where his grave is located. (1977)

Mansfield Mill Marker
Location: 100 E. Broad Street in Mansfield

Julian Feild (1825-1897) and Ralph Mann (1825-1906) became acquainted in Harrison County, Texas, about 1850. About 1854 they built a mill near the Clear and West Forks of the Trinity River.

The two business partners came south of Fort Worth in 1856 and at this site found the ruins of a mill that had been constructed by Charles Turner. With the help of local settlers and brick makers, S.W.A. Hook (1836-1917), Mann and Feild built a three–story steam-powered corn mill during the winter of 1859-60.

The mill attracted business from San Antonio to the Oklahoma Territory. The community that developed around the mill was given the name "Mansfeild" (now Mansfield). During the Civil War, the Confederate government collected for its use a certain proportion of the mill's output. After the war, government contracts were secured to supply flour for federal forts. Julian Feild sold his interest in the mill in 1874. Ralph Man remained active in the business until 1894. The mill continued in operation until the early part of the 20th century. The site has been used since that time as a memorial to World War I veterans and for municipal offices. It is a historic site as the beginning of the city of Mansfield. (1895)

John C. Collier Home Marker
Location: 401 E. Elm Street, Mansfield.

This structure was built in 1877 as a residence for the founder of Mansfield Male and Female College, John C. Collier (1834-1928). A native of South Carolina, Collier was a distinguished educator and Presbyterian minister who in 1869 was asked to establish a school in Mansfield. The college operated from 1870 until 1887 and produced outstanding graduates and community leaders.

Located west of the college, the home served also as a residence for female teachers and students. From 1890 to 1909, the A.J. Dukes family owned the Collier house. They made some major alterations to the home, including the addition of Mansfield's first indoor bathroom.

Occupants of the home from 1909 until 1944 were Dr. William B. and Sallie (Hodges) McKnight, both of whom had graduated from Mansfield Male and Female College. Dr. McKnight established a medical practice in Mansfield in 1895 and also served as physician for the Southern Pacific Railroad. The house was adapted as Mansfield's first funeral home by T.E. "Ernie" Blessing in 1944.

Significant for its association with an early Texas educational

155

institution and with several families of community leaders, the John C. Collier Home has remained a landmark in Mansfield. (1985)

Nugent-Hart House Marker

Location: 312 Waxahachie Street, Mansfield.

Nugent-Hart House: In the early 1890s Joseph Nugent (1829-1903) and his wife, Christina, built this house, which features late 19th-century Victorian and Eastlake details in the porch.

Nugent, a native of Canada, came to Texas in 1851. He operated a private school in Mansfield in the 1850s, taught at the Mansfield Male and Female College, and was elected the first Mayor in 1891. Local farmer J.H. Hart bought the home in 1920, and it was later inherited by family members.

Cross Timbers Marker

Location: 2602 Mayfield Road, Grand Prairie.

This narrow strip of sandy timberland, called "The Eastern Cross Timbers", separates the Blackland Prairie and the Grand Prairie. It covers about one million acres. Indians camped here because the mild climate, good soil, frequent rains and nearby prairies supported large herds of buffalo and horses. There were salt licks, fresh water springs, trees for fuel, and good grass. They also found game for food and hides. West of the Grand Prairie, covering about 2.7 million acres, is "The Western Cross Timbers." During the 18th century Wichita Indians, of Caddoan stock roamed this area. Southern plains tribes, such as the Kiowa and the Comanche, often wintered here and traded with them. Cultural exchanges occurred here as trade routes developed between flint sources in the south and tribes from the north. By 1720 French traders came. They opened the trading posts and bartered with the Indians. The Spanish moved through, traveling to their Mission outposts. Settlement in the 1840s by Anglo-Americans led to clashes. A turning point came on May 24, 1841, with the battle of Village Creek, a few miles west of this site.

The Indians withdrew to the west, leaving the land to the white settlers. (1979)

Marion Loyd Homestead Marker
Location: Inside Loyd Park off Ragland Road near the Loyd Park entrance, Grand Prairie.

In 1859 brothers Marion (1835-1927) and James Loyd (1837-1922) of Illinois purchased this site. Marion built a log house to which their father John and several younger children came to live. Marion married Friendsina Cheshier (1841-1870) in 1862 and had four children. In 1879 he married his brother Thomas' (1848-1873) widow Ann Haney Loyd (1853-1912) and had three children. Marion was a farmer, area leader, and organizer of Loyd school. His deep soft water well made his home a gathering place for neighbors and travelers. *Loyd descendants remain on the land. (1980)

Note: Much of the Loyd property became park property when Joe Pool Lake was created by the Corps of Engineers. The park is now part of the Grand Prairie park system.

Wilson Cemetery Marker
Location: Lake Ridge Parkway, Grand Prairie; across from entrance of Lynn Creek Park at Joe Pool lake. (requires a quarter-mile walk on an abandoned road that dead-ends into the lake.)

This pioneer cemetery dates to 1872, when Charles N. Wilson buried his wife and infant child here. Ophelia E. West Wilson (1853-1872) and her newborn daughter died as a result of complications during childbirth. The third grave in the cemetery, that of the Bowlin infant, is unmarked. James W. and Mattie C. Bowlin buried their son here, since a public graveyard was not readily accessible to their home. The Wilson Cemetery contains only these three graves, but it is an important reminder of the ways of life in 19th century Tarrant County. Texas Sesquicentennial 1836-1986

Note: Most geological references call the "Grand Prairie" the Eagle Ford. It is the Eastern Cross Timbers that crosses through this area. The Western Cross Timbers is a more hilly geological strata about 80 miles west.

The Hill

Location: George Stevens Park, Arlington, Texas Historical Marker 400 W Sanford St, Arlington, TX

A roughly five-block area of Arlington known as "The Hill" was the only addition specifically set aside for the city's African-American residents. In the 1890s, the community began developing on land that once belonged to Martin V. and Rebecca A. Thomas.

Several churches organized in the emerging community. The Church of God in Christ, Mt. Olive Baptist Church and the African Methodist Episcopal (AME) Church, now known as Armstrong Chapel AME, became leading institutions in the neighborhood. Mt. Olive, in particular, became a center for spiritual life while also hosting many community and social events. In 1907, Arlington resident Edward F. Wilkerson subdivided land known as the Wilkerson Addition that became the core of The Hill. Growth occurred in the following years as a vibrant community emerged including grocery stores, clubs and restaurants opening by the 1920s.

Other important institutions included a school, which the county first established for Arlington's African American children in the 1890s. The last segregated school in The Hill, named for Booker T. Washington, was built in 1953 and closed as integration took place in the 1960s.

Another vital part of the neighborhood was this park, opened by the city in the mid-1950s and named for George Stevens, principal of Booker T. Washington School. Although The Hill was originally a rural community, it became more densely populated and urban as the city grew out to meet it by the 1930s. From the mid-1940s through the 1960s,

The Hill began to decline as job opportunities and social changes led residents to other areas. Today, The Hill has become an ethnically diverse community. (2006)

Booker T. Washington

Location: 500 Houston St, Arlington, TX The Marker Wording for the Booker T. Washington Elementary School.

Serving the African-American students of Arlington, Booker T. Washington School was a vital institution in the city. It had its roots in Arlington's first black school which was in place by the 1890s. The school served the growing African-American community known as the Hill, located northwest of the original town boundaries. The Church of God in Christ provided class space as needed.

In 1902, the school became a part of the newly formed Arlington Independent School District. George Stevens and Gloria Echols were appointed teachers, with Stevens also serving as principal. Both lived in the neighborhood and are noted for their impact in the lives of their young students. The original school building was replaced after a severe 1903 storm. Students attended the school through the eighth grade and then they went to I. M. Terrell in Fort Worth.

A new facility opened at 500 Houston Street in 1954, named Booker T. Washington. The building had eight classrooms, an administration office and cafeteria. A gymnasium was added later. George Stevens continued as principal of the institution. In 1965, schools began full desegregation. Booker T. Washington closed and became Veda Knox School, a facility for students with special educational needs. It later became the Metro Math and Science Academy. Today, Booker T. Washington School is remembered as an iconic institution in The Hill providing students with skills and education to help them achieve success in their personal and professional lives. (2010)

Chapter 9 – Entertainment

Arlington contains a plethora of assets, but perhaps inescapably it has a national and even international brand—an out-of-towner's idea of what the city is about: It's a brand that brings up visions of roller coasters, water slides, home runs and long touchdown passes. It's a brand that's constantly reinforced with every trip a motorist makes through the city along Interstate 30 and with every televised Texas Rangers or Dallas Cowboys game—a brand made anew with every Cotton Bowl, which the city now hosts.

There is, of course, much more to the city than its visitor attractions, but there's no denying that Arlington has evolved over the years into an amusements and professional sports Mecca of enviable proportions unequalled by any other Texas city. Six Flags Over Texas Amusement Park has long been the state's top commercial attraction. Hurricane Harbor, a Six Flags-owned water park, pulls in hundreds of thousands of visitors.

Hurricane Harbor

The city also is host to Major League Baseball's Texas Rangers and most recently became home to the world's most valuable sports franchise, the Dallas Cowboys of the National Football League. Arlington is clearly an entertainment and visitation industry powerhouse. The collective economic and cultural impact is difficult to measure. Six Flags has brought in more than 100 million park goers over its half-century history. The Texas Rangers, a team that went to the World Series in 2010, was on track for close to three million in attendance in 2011. The Cowboys consistently sell out every game in a stadium capable of holding 100,000—the world's largest indoor sports venue. And the team's new Arlington stadium also hosts an ongoing series of non-Cowboys events ranging from the National Basketball Association All-Star Game and Cotton Bowl to hosting the Super Bowl in 2011. Throw in concerts and other events and the stadium is an immense attraction for dollar-spending visitors, albeit one with a degree of taxpayer support a consideration that has historically not occurred without political controversy either with the Rangers or the Cowboys.

The city's collective success in amassing so many high-dollar, high-profile attractions certainly begs a question: How did Arlington pull it off?

The city's location in the midst of the Metroplex—an area more populous than 25 states—certainly helps, as does access via two interstate highways. There's also the advantage of synergy. The success of Six Flags made the possibility of attracting sufficient fans for major league baseball to what was then perceived as a suburban community more viable. The Rangers' success was no doubt critical to the eventual decision by Cowboys' ownership to move the football team to the city.

While the basics of attraction—location, accessibility and sufficient population—had to exist, it could also be argued that two other factors had to be present for Arlington to become such a tourism giant: Capable and energetic leadership had to be present at the right time, and the electorate had to be prepared to offer taxpayer support when requested for the city to attract and keep both the Rangers and Cowboys by helping fund new facilities. Finding that blend of leadership and community support in a city Arlington's size is not easy, though the community's history of tourism– it once hosted both a horse racing track and a casino—might have helped establish an accommodating mindset.

That being noted, Arlington's foray into the amusements and professional sports industry began with a desperate attempt to save a floundering industrial district.

Six Flags Over Texas

In the spring of 1958 a dozen men sat brainstorming in a small office in northeast Arlington. A grand vision, the Great Southwest Industrial District, was a giant in land area but small in actual development and awash in red ink. The fledgling warehouse and manufacturing park, which included what is now the site of Six Flags Over Texas, was not full of manufacturers and warehouses. Instead it was covered with horse barns, grazing cattle and cotton fields being consumed by ragweed and Johnson grass. Great with potential, but slow in development, the district stretched across ten square miles of Arlington and Grand Prairie.

Developer Angus Wynne II, his brother Toddie, and investors William Zekendorf Sr. and William Zekendorf Jr. had used up both cash and credit to buy the land, with other investors including a member of the Rockefeller family. Their purchase included the local W.T. Waggoner Ranch, site of the old Arlington Downs Racetrack, and almost 7,000 acres surrounding it—potentially one of the largest planned industrial districts in the nation. But with only two warehouses paying rent—and costly rail lines, roads and water lines yet to be installed—the men faced a problem.

"They needed cash, lots of it, to finance the industrial park's development," said then-Arlington Mayor Tom Vandergriff, who was present that fateful "what'll we do to save this thing" day.

At a break, someone started talking about Disneyland and then someone else—Vandergriff said it might have been Wynne himself—made a joke about creating an amusement park to generate funds. Wynne, who had never been to Disneyland, seemed not to take the idea seriously—at first.

"But when he left the meeting, he commented it was an idea worth considering," Vandergriff recalled in a 1994 interview.

But Wynne, having first thought the amusement park idea was a whimsical stretch, found himself increasingly focusing on the amusement park idea. He visited Disneyland soon afterward and liked what he saw with a single exception. He returned convinced that an amusement park would work. The single exception? He didn't like the idea that people paid to get into Disneyland and then paid again for rides. He preferred a pay once, ride free concept.

Wynne, taken with the idea of Texas having been around under six different national flags (Mexico, Spain, France, Texas Republic, Confederacy and the U.S.) based on a small decoration on his son's desk, originally meant to call the park "Six Flags Under Texas" until his wife – a member of the Daughters of the Republic of Texas— reminded him that Texas wasn't "under" anything. It became Six Flags Over Texas.

Wynne hired Hollywood set maker Randall Duell to design the park on the site of a vacant dairy farm, construction of which began in 1960. Duell had been an art director on 65 films and had been nominated for several academy awards, though he was most famous for helping design the sets for "Singin' in the Rain."

"He (Duell) could look at a cornfield and be able to see how he wanted everything laid out," said Dean Dauley, the first manager of Six Flags. Duell designed the park so that there were no dead ends, but with each turn, Dauley said, "promising a new excitement."

The park opened Aug. 5, 1961, at a cost of $3.4 million—less than many of the new rides would cost to construct in years to come. Response exceeded both Wynne and Vandergriff's expectations. They had hit the tourism equivalent to a gusher.

"The original park was more successful than anyone visualized, so much so that when the first crowd of 10,000 showed up, we had to issue appeals to area radio and TV stations not to come to Six Flags that day," park publicist Bruce Neal said in an early 1990s recollection.

"At one point we even had to open the park to any food vendors that wanted to come in just to take care of demand."

The park paid for itself promptly and soon began providing a flood of cash for the original purpose—putting the Great Southwest Industrial Park on a firm financial foundation.

"It paid off all its construction cost and made a profit the first year," said Dauley, the park's general manager for the first ten years of existence. "Without the park, I'm not sure the district wouldn't have been a flop."

Six Flags Over Texas

"It paid off all its construction cost and made a profit the first year," said Dauley, the park's general manager for the first ten years of existence. "Without the park, I'm not sure the district wouldn't have been a flop."

Dauley said the park surged, using its $5 million annual profits to build infrastructure and other elements for the industrial park. Though Wynne originally envisioned the park as being around for only about ten years, it instead survived and became the prototype for a chain of similar parks around the country. Six Flags also quickly established itself as Arlington's signature brand industry, demonstrating that the spot equidistant to Fort Worth and Dallas was an ideal location for entertainment amenities—for example a future professional baseball or football team.

"The trip lever for it all, and not coincidentally for much of Arlington's industrial development, was Six Flags," Dauley said. "The park attracted hotel and restaurant development and its success helped attract Wet 'n Wild (now Hurricane Harbor), the Texas Rangers and the Palace of Wax in Grand Prairie."

It could easily be argued that it was the amusement park, more so than the General Motors plant or the University of Texas at Arlington— or being the fastest growing city in the nation for a couple of decades— that gave Arlington its first real state and national identity. Tourism for Arlington became what oil was to Odessa—what cattle once was to Fort Worth and what banking was to Dallas. All of it, in the beginning, was neither planned nor expected.

"We thought of the usual things in economic development like bringing industry and housing or of getting UTA to four-year status, but never in our wildest fantasies did we consider the possibility of Arlington becoming a tourist Mecca," Vandergriff—by then a former congressman and sitting county judge— said in a 1990's conversation. "When it came, it came out of the blue. The original park was far more sedate than today's (rollercoaster-oriented) version. There were stage coach and river boat rides, conventional amusement park rides, an Astrolift that gave patrons an aerial view, a Fiesta train and petting zoo, and an amphitheater for outdoor entertainers, a concept that was to prove increasingly important as Six Flags sought to attract a slightly older audience."

Wynne had financial problems not related to Six Flags or the industrial park, eventually losing control of both by 1971. Penn Central, which bought controlling interest from Wynne, sold the park chain to Bally Manufacturing in 1982. Several other parks were built in the nation based on the Arlington prototype. Six Flags executives eventually bought the corporation, in turn to sell out to Time-Warner by 1992.

Major stockholders have since produced other changes in ownership and operation. The current owner, Six Flag Entertainment Corp., operates 14 amusement parks and recently emerged from a 2009 bankruptcy. About 120 individuals, including many of Wynne's heirs, own the land upon which the Arlington Six Flags rests, leasing it to park operators.

Over time the Arlington attraction has increasingly focused on thrill rides, associations with movie characters like Batman and Bugs Bunny, and on a steady stream of highly popular celebrity musicians providing concerts.

Texas Rangers

The odds of a city of 100,000 attracting a Major League Baseball team would seem to be astronomically opposed, but nevertheless that was about the city's population when the Texas Rangers—formerly the Washington Senators—relocated to the city in 1972.

The issue wasn't so much population because to be in Arlington was to be in the middle of the booming Metroplex, tapping into a couple of million people within a 30-minute travel circle. The big issue in attracting major sports teams tends to be economic resources because such franchises rarely show up without requiring an assortment of costly incentives from their governmental host.

Sometimes not even wealth helps in such an endeavor. Multi-millionaire Lamar Hunt, for example, had tried to attract a baseball franchise to the Dallas area in the mid-1960s and failed, even with his enormous resources.

But longtime Arlington Mayor Tom Vandergriff had begun talking about the viability of an MLB team located in Arlington as early as the late 1950s, an idea that was not treated with a great deal of respect initially either by MLB or the big money Dallas or Fort Worth crowd. Vandergriff was, however, able to influence the construction of a minor league ballpark in Arlington in 1965.

Initially called Turnpike Stadium, it was named after the adjoining toll road, now Interstate 30. The stadium seated about 10,000 and was home to the Fort Worth Cats, followed by the Texas League Dallas-Fort Worth Spurs. The stadium field—essentially a sunken bowl—was designed to meet major league standards and metal seating could be expanded. By 1970 the field accommodated 20,500 fans and had a reputation as both the noisiest field—thousands of feet slamming metal floors could be heard for miles—and the hottest in the country.

Though Hunt's failure to attract a team was a setback, Vandergriff continued to look for opportunities and in 1971 began focusing on the financially troubled Washington Senators, then owned by Bob Short. Short's team was consistently one of the worst performers in baseball, typically losing 90 or more games a year. With attendance and fan enthusiasm understandably lagging, the owner also had a severe cash flow problem that required a near-$10 million infusion. Vandergriff offered both a ballpark for the Senators—then managed by baseball legend Ted Williams—and the $10 million via a 10-year lease of radio and TV broadcast rights. Vandergriff did not have time to secure voter approval for his endeavor—a risk of major proportions—and even had to have his father, W.T. "Hooker" Vandergriff, accept a million dollars' worth of risk.

Short was desperate and accepted the proposal, though there were issues that had to be overcome in both MLB and politics, with President Richard Nixon appealing to Vandergriff to leave the team in Washington. Security guards walked off in protest during the team's last game in Washington, and more than 10,000 unhappy fans walked in, resulting in a forfeit to the New York Yankees because referees refused to allow play without security.

Seating capacity at Turnpike Stadium was increased to 35,700 after the 1972 season, including the highest percentage of bleacher seating in baseball. The facility was renamed Arlington Stadium and the Rangers settled for many years into a recurring pattern of modest success followed by a return to mediocrity. Periodically, a new ownership group—Brad Corbett, Eddie Chiles and others—would take control of the team. By the late 1990s the team was faring better, winning West Division championships in 1996, 1998 and 1999, and playing for the first time in the World Series in 2010, losing to the San Francisco Giants. The team repeated as division champions in 2011.

As might be expected, the team quickly grew disenchanted with what was essentially a revamped minor league field and a new ownership group put together by George W. Bush proposed to either have a new field built or potentially move the franchise elsewhere within the Metroplex.

Voters in 1991, with the endorsement and leadership of then-Mayor Richard Greene, approved by a near 2-1 margin a half-cent sales tax to fund $135 million of a $165 million ballpark, though the Rangers eventually spent slightly more for their share. The last game at Arlington Stadium was Oct. 3, 1993, a 4-1 loss to the Kansas City Royals. The Rangers moved to the Ballpark in Arlington in 1994, and old Arlington Stadium was demolished.

George Bush's investor group eventually sold their interest in the team to Tom Hicks, also the owner of the Dallas Stars hockey team. Bush went on to become governor of Texas and president of the United States. He still regularly attends Rangers games.

When Hicks began suffering financial problems, an ownership group led by former Rangers pitcher Nolan Ryan and sports entrepreneur Chuck Greenberg purchased the team in 2010—the team making its first World Series that year. Greenberg's tenure was brief, his interest being bought out by the team before the 2011 season.

Rangers Ballpark

The Ballpark in Arlington was renamed to Ameriquest Field in Arlington in 2004 and the name changed again to Rangers Ballpark in

2006. Roofless and featuring natural grass, the field is still considered the warmest venue in MLB—summer "first pitch" games can start at 100 degrees or more—but is also viewed as a hitter's park. The majority of games are played in the evening. Seating capacity is 49,200.

Dallas Cowboys

The decision by the Dallas Cowboys—one of the most valuable professional sports franchises on the planet—to replace Texas Stadium in Irving with a new indoor facility in Arlington might well be considered by urban sociologists to be a premium example of the realities of opportunity costs.

Basically, opportunity cost translates to the idea that if someone— or a city—decides to spend a dollar or millions of dollars on something, it means the opportunity to make an investment with those funds in something else has been lost. It's essentially a cost-benefit consideration.

Arlington voters, for instance, on three occasions over the years have rejected the idea of funding mass transit with a local sales tax, the result being that the city is now the only municipality among the 100 most populous cities in the country without a mass transit system. Likewise, voters in recent years turned down a similar sales tax funding mechanism for what would have converted Johnson Creek into a giant, green space linear park. Arlington also turned out to be one of the few cities in which voters bounced a sales tax-funded crime district.

If, somewhere along the way, voters had approved mass transit funding from sales tax proceeds, it would have meant that the dollars voters approved for a new Texas Rangers ballpark would not have been available. It only took eleven years for the Rangers debt to be paid off (far ahead of schedule), which left the half cent sales tax available again for other uses, such as mass transit or the crime district or for something else—ideas that were consistently rejected until the Cowboys came along. Clearly, there's something about attracting sports franchises that deeply appeals to Arlington voters, even in preference to such amenities as mass transit, park systems and crime prevention.

Even so, most urban prognosticators would not have predicted that the Dallas Cowboys would eventually end up in Arlington. That it ended up doing so hinged not so much on Arlington's early efforts but on the combination of economic realities and the political atmosphere of Dallas County in the late 1990s and early 2000s. When Cowboys owner Jerry Jones began campaigning for a new state-of-the-art indoor stadium he ran up against the hard side of the opportunity costs equation in Irving right away. The city had invested its excess sales tax dollars in membership in the Dallas Area Regional Transit (DART) and simply didn't have the resources to fund a new stadium.

Jones found in the persons of then-Dallas Mayor Laura Miller and County Commissioner John Wiley Price two powerful political figures who were not enthusiastic about the possibility of extensive governmental investment in Jones' vision. While not an impossible task, the complexities of financing and the balancing act required were probably perceived by Jones as increasingly daunting.

But meanwhile in Arlington, in 2003, councilman and soon-to-be-elected Mayor Robert Cluck, a physician, was fretting about the city's economic condition.

"I thought Arlington was in trouble," Cluck said. "We were stagnant, and there was not much new economic activity. I strongly felt that we needed to go out and get something big for Arlington. I knew the Cowboys were looking. That's why I asked Jerry (Jones) if he would talk to me about it."

That first conversation between the two on the stadium topic was by phone from Mexico, where the Cowboys were playing an exhibition game. But, after that, the relationship and the number of meetings between the two began to escalate. Eventually, when Dallas talks bogged down and Jones scaled back his expectation, he gave Cluck a dollar number: He thought the stadium would cost about $650 million.

"I told him we were good for half of it," Cluck recalled.

"Dallas didn't have the component of a great leader," Jones later said. "I found that leadership in Bob Cluck and that great Arlington City Council."

Though speculation ran rampant that Jones was simply using Arlington to apply leverage to Dallas—certainly a possibility—in the summer of 2004 the Cowboys owner and Cluck shook hands on a deal that had yet to be approved by Arlington voters. With voter endorsement the city would guarantee $325 million, and absolutely no more. But there was a snag. A survey of Arlington residents indicated that almost two out of three potential voters had misgivings about the deal.

Historically in Arlington, most such elections are scheduled to be local events only, but the city decided to use the 2004 November national election day, which meant that instead of the usual 10,000 or so local voters participating the turnout would be more than 100,000. Meanwhile, advocates of the stadium ran an intensive and expensive campaign, with opponents bringing in a number of economists who cited various studies noting the limited economic impact of professional sports franchises on local economies. A Star-Telegram survey conducted shortly before the election indicated that the public attitude had changed somewhat in favor of the stadium, but it was still a close call.

Deal Basics: The city would raise three taxes to fund the facility, a half-cent sales tax, a rental car tax increase of five percent and a two percent increase on hotel room taxes. The city would own the Cowboys complex and lease it for a base rent of $2 million annually, plus the city would be entitled to five percent of naming rights up to $500,000 yearly. The Cowboys would also invest $16.5 million—$500,000 annually—in a youth recreational program. The city would also impose a user tax of 10 percent on admission tickets and a $3 parking tax for each vehicle.

About 107,000 people showed up for the election, by far the largest vote on a local issue in the city's history. Some 62,000 of them—58 percent—voted yes. On a national basis the overwhelming victory was one of the most substantial in favor of a sports venue in the nation's history.

The controversy would not end there. The city would eventually have to purchase almost 200 private properties, sometimes agreeably with owners and sometimes through condemnation, spreading across 134 acres immediately southwest of the Texas Rangers ballpark. The city offered an appraisal-plus consideration, plus a moving costs payment. Apartment residents also received a moving costs payment.

Legislative actions had to be taken to refine and legalize some components of the agreement, and transportation and access issues had to be addressed. The primary considerations included a revamping of four interchanges on Interstate 30 and a rework of a section of State Highway 360, where traffic was often constricted because of a railroad bridge that narrowed traffic. From Arlington's $325 million investment, the city paid more than $79.5 million to acquire and demolish 162 properties, including 51 businesses, 927 apartment units, and 105 single-family homes, plus more than $4 million for 1,083 relocations.

Cowboys Stadium

The completed Cowboys Stadium contained 22,000 tons of steel, nearly 2,000 concrete columns rising 10 stories into the air, more than 225,000 cubic yards of concrete overall, and half a million square feet of glass and stone. By the first quarter of 2007, the stadium began rising like a Phoenix from the bowl. The stadium was built in layers, and construction moved in a counter-clockwise direction as each layer was added.

"Every day something changed that would impact the residents in the area," said Gerald Urbantke, Arlington's communications manager. "Our job was to inform citizens what was going to happen, how long it would take, and how it would impact them."

In July of 2007, two cranes lifted the first section of steel into place, the beginnings of the quarter mile arch that would support the largest single-span roof structure in the world, a technique similar to bridge construction. The arches could be seen from six miles away. A second arch supported both the retractable roof and the world's largest video scoreboard.

Though Arlington's investment was capped at $325 million, Jones' investment was limited only by his resources. The stadium eventually could cost almost $1.2 billion and would be the largest indoor arena in the world.

The stadium was completed in May of 2009 and it quickly became evident that Jones had far more uses in mind than professional football. Jones quickly scheduled concerts with performers like George Strait, Paul McCartney and U2, along with events like the NBA All-Star Game and boxing matches featuring pugilists like Manny Pacquiao. The Cotton Bowl opted to play at the stadium and a number of high profile college football games were scheduled.

Though the event was marred by a once-in-20-years ice storm, the stadium hosted the 2011 Super Bowl Game—the first of what is likely to be many such events. Collectively the stadium will host more than 100 events a year as well as other smaller venues. The first game played in the team's new home was a preseason match with the Tennessee Titans in August 2009.

Cluck has made it clear that the stadium exceeds even his expectations.

"Over the years some venues (in Arlington) have come and gone, but our Entertainment District has continued to grow and evolve in ways many could not have imagined," he said in remarks made a year after the opening. "With the addition of Cowboys Stadium, that tradition continues. Its positive impact, both culturally and economically is evident. I feel this venue was a tipping point in Arlington's history, and we now find ourselves with a permanent global presence and a reliable source of revenue for the city."

Seven Seas

Though Arlington may appear to have a charmed life when it came to tourist and sports attractions, there have been setbacks. The legislature zapped the highly profitable Arlington Downs Racetrack in the 1930s in a snit about the evils of gambling in the midst of both the Bible Belt and the Great Depression. And the law finally got around to shutting down another highly profitable but illegal activity in the 1940s, the Top 'O Hill Casino.

But the city's greatest setback in the modern era would have to be the failure of Seven Seas, a city-owned marine theme park that opened in 1971.

Then-Mayor Tom Vandergriff persuaded voters to fund a 40-acre park somewhat akin to Japanese Village and Sea World at San Diego. The park would feature all kinds of performing marine animals divided into seven sections and about 25 exhibits, in tandem with a seafood restaurant. A lagoon featured divers and the showpieces were a 1,200-seat auditorium featuring dolphins, along with a killer whale tank filled with 700,000 gallons of water. The park's star attraction would eventually turn out to be Newtka the killer whale.

Vandergriff introduced the idea in 1970, and though there was opposition, voters did approve a $10 million bond issue by a three-to-one majority in a May 1970 ballot. The park was to be operated by the Great Southwest Corp., the same operators as Six Flags. Though the park had a few ride attractions, the general idea was to compliment Six Flags and make Arlington a multi-day destination.

Problems began almost immediately; starting with the sudden bankruptcy of Penn Central, owners of Great Southwest Corp. GSC subsequently withdrew, leaving the city to operate the park itself. Along the way the city had to both defend itself in court and to ask legislators to fine tune state regulations. The city also decided in late 1971 to create the Arlington Park Corporation to operate the park as a non-profit organization, freeing the council and city staff from having to directly manage the facility. The APC would also run the Texas Rangers Radio and TV Network—the city having purchased the rights for 10 years as part of an accommodation to help Rangers owner Bob Short with his financial difficulties. Though the park reported a modest profit of about $80,000 at the end of its first season, the broadcast network lost more than half a million dollars.

The park debuted with a municipal parade and opened ahead of schedule, March 18, 1972, though $2 million over budget at $9 million. Tickets were $2.75 for children, $3.75 for adults. The park's sections included the Arctic Ocean, Mediterranean Sea, Sea of Cortez, Sea of Japan, Caribbean Sea, Indian Ocean and South Sea. Attendance was initially promising. The park had 80,000 visitors from 41 states and 5 countries in its first 50 days, though a recurring problem had not yet surfaced. The marine animal acts were somewhat fixed and changed only with difficulty. And the number of entertainment rides was minimal, which meant that many people felt there was no need to return after a trip or two.

Indeed, attendance began slumping during the 1973 season, with the city also being forced to issue more than $8 million in certificates of indebtedness to, in effect, repurchase debt from the APC. The total losses that season, including bond debt and the broadcast network losses, was about $1.3 million—significant for a city Arlington's size at the time.

When a deal to have Sea World take over the park fell through, Vandergriff fashioned an agreement with Six Flags to run Seven Seas. Six Flags successfully ran the park at a profit for the 1974 season but the earnings were not sufficient to pay the park's steadily increasing debt load. Arlington Park Corporation and Leisure Marine Corp ran the park the next year, then Leisure Marine declined to renew the lease. J&L Enterprises took over the park in 1976, renaming it as Hawaii Kai.

Unfortunately, in September of that year J&L filed for bankruptcy, by which time the city's original investment in the marine park had blossomed from $10 million to $41 million.

Having gone through five operators, the city council had enough. Members in December of 1976 voted unanimously to get out of the amusement park business. The park animals and other resources were auctioned. A later council would convert part of the area to parking for the Texas Rangers and the new Arlington Convention Center, and some of the space would be sold to the Sheraton Hotel, which today still uses the Seven Seas pearl diving pool as a hotel facility. The Seven Seas era was over.

In the 1980s a new water park, Wet 'n Wild, would be built on the other side of Interstate 30 from the original site of Seven Seas. Wet 'n Wild, which would feature elaborate water features like slide and surf machines, but zero marine attractions, would be very successful, eventually being purchased by Six Flags and renamed as Hurricane Harbor Six Flags. It remains an attraction today, attracting hundreds of thousands of visitors during its six month season.

Hurricane Harbor

Chapter 10 – Transportation and Access

Accessibility and transportation amenities are important for every city, access to transportation often—as in "always"—being a make-or-break situation. This was true in Arlington's pioneer days and the impact has grown even more significant in this century and the last.

Two topographical realities contributed greatly to Arlington being one of the first cities settled in this region of Texas, those being the Eastern Cross Timbers and the Trinity River. The Eastern Cross Timbers is a narrow band of oak-timbered land typically no wider than 15 miles and often narrower. From the eastern half of Cooke County it extends southward through the eastern parts of Denton, Tarrant and Johnson counties and the western parts of Grayson, Dallas, Ellis and Hill counties. It includes the hilly western segment of Arlington and the Eastern Cross Timbers finally disappearing west of Waco. Several branches of the Trinity merge near Fort Worth and the river, essentially flowing eastward before turning south at Dallas, runs through the northern section of Arlington. Prairie, which millions of years ago was a shallow sea, is on both sides.

Caddo Indians used the edge of the Cross Timbers as a trade route, a fact not lost on early frontiersmen. Navigating the vast reaches of Texas could be incredibly difficult, particularly when crossing hundreds of square miles of prairie that all appeared extremely similar because it was, after all, a sea of grass. But those frontiersmen developed a handy trick. All they had to do was find either the 200-mile long edge of the Cross Timbers and follow it to the Trinity River, or find the Trinity and follow it to the edge of the Cross Timbers. That confluence of the Trinity and Cross Timbers, for example, was the location of the first attempted settlement in Arlington, Bird's Fort. And it was not a coincidence that the first successful settlement, Johnson Station, is located on Johnson Creek (present day Mayfield Road east of Cooper Street) in what is now mid Arlington. The creek happens to be both a tributary of the Trinity River and also the break point between the Eastern Cross Timbers and Eagle Ford Prairie.

The nuances of such navigation became less important as trails became easy-to-follow wagon roads that later would become paved road. The wandering of South Center Street, for example, began as just such a wagon trail, as did Matlock Road.

Almost as soon as Col. Middleton Tate Johnson arrived at what would become Johnson Station in 1848 (originally Kaufman Station and then Marrow Bone Spring Post) the station and surrounding areas began to be served by the Star Mail Route and Truck Stage Coach line.

Texas and Pacific Railway

Texas and Pacific Railway

Once prospering, on a small scale at least, Johnson Station eventually disappeared because of another mode of transportation that would be located a few miles north—the Texas and Pacific Railway.

Though horsepower and wagons work efficiently enough for a pioneer environment, true commerce requires a faster and more efficient transportation system. In 1871 the Congress granted a charter for a transcontinental railroad system, with a route to come through Texas. The contract to build the railroad into Fort Worth from Dallas was signed in 1874, a process delayed by a financial panic that slowed the sale of railroad bonds. Nevertheless, surveying for the railroad continued with the railroad literally establishing small stop points along the way, laying out the future streets of future communities in the process. Texas and Pacific planners had determined they needed such a stop midway between Fort Worth and Dallas. The community they surveyed for this purpose had Main and Center streets at its center and would soon be called Arlington. The first T&P Engine, No. 20, rolled into Arlington early on the morning of July 19, 1876. The first blast of the locomotive horn by the train engineer effectively signaled the end of the pioneer era. The Old West would have moved further west.

Arlington would soon have a small station and regular passenger and freight service. Cotton gins—and saloons, churches and retail businesses—would spring up all around the station as a town newly created by the iron horse rose from surveyors' stakes. Many residents of nearby communities would swiftly shut the doors on their cabins and move to Arlington. The town would officially incorporate in 1884. A newspaper, the Arlington World, would come into being in 1883. James Ditto would become the town's first postmaster. I.L. Hutcheson would shutter his doors at Johnson Station and move near the rails. Col. Abram Harris would conduct the first Union Sunday School in the train depot. William McNatt would move all the way from Arkansas with his family so that he could open a general mercantile store in Arlington. Merchant Rice Wood Collins would be so persuasive in extolling this new place's merits that he would soon be joined by his brothers Marshall, Tom (a future mayor) and Joseph. By 1900 the town would blossom from zero to about 1,000 residents. In time the presence of the railroad would prove to be an invaluable asset that would make it possible to attract commerce like the Great Southwest Industrial District or General Motors. Such is the power of the right kind of transportation.

But that kind of development would take a while. As if the presence of the railroad powered by steam engines were not enough, transportation powered by electricity would soon become a factor in Arlington's development.

A July 4, 1901, editorial by Arlington Journal Editor Harry Johnson proclaimed that Arlington needed three things: "An electric light plant, water works system and fire company, well organized," he wrote.

"Arlington also needs more rent houses. There is not a vacant rent house in the city, and the demand for them is increasing steadily."

Interurban Line

Interurban Depot

Johnson would soon get all of his wishes, aided in part by the catalytic power of the Northern Traction Company and its newest Interurban line. The route would connect Fort Worth to Dallas by running right through the middle of Arlington on what is now Abram Street, starting June 19, 1902. That first Interurban was clocked at the then-blinding speed of 54 miles an hour, which meant that the arrival of a single bit of technology—essentially a speedy street car— had changed what was an all-day buggy ride from Arlington to Fort Worth or Dallas to about a half hour. The Interurban would also enable the first hints of a future phenomenon—the suburban commuter who could live in a place like Arlington but work elsewhere.

The Interurban would be an Arlington fixture until the mid-1930s, shutting down finally—the last trip took place on Christmas Eve 1934— because it was replaced by yet another popular transportation innovation, the automobile, which by itself gradually ratcheted up the demand for more streets and more highways.

Nevertheless, there is this reality: Transportation in the form of the railroad and then the Interurban sprang Arlington forth from a pasture on the prairie. Consider this editorial by Arlington Journal Editor Laten Stanberry from August 1902:

"Arlington now has: One railroad, one electric line with fifty-two trains in constant daily passage; one oil mill; two square and one round (cotton) bale gins with twenty-eight gin stands in the three of them; four rural delivery routes with the establishment of nine more expected; one national bank; five dry goods stores; three hardware stores; eight grocery stores; four saloons but since the town voted dry, they are to go out of business within thirty days; two livery stables; two meat markets; four cold drink stands; two lumber yards; one jewelry store; eight doctors; one saddle and harness shop; three barber shops; two telephone systems with two exchanges; two restaurants; four blacksmith shops; one shoe shop; one paint shop; one general repair shop and one flour mill."

Stanberry went on to include The Carlisle School for Boys—one of the many names for what would eventually become UT Arlington—on the city's list of assets. In 26 short years the city had emerged from surveyors' stakes along a future railroad line to a bustling village of more than 1,000 that had quickly evolved into a popular destination for farmers to convert their cotton and wheat to marketable commodities that would be purchased and shipped via the railroad throughout the nation. The town had grown so quickly that, Stanberry noted, a half dozen families a week were being turned away from the city because there were no houses to rent.

"If we had twenty or thirty new houses right now they would be filled within a few weeks," Stanberry said of the city's agrarian business boom. "All kinds of businesses would flourish thereby."

Good Roads Movement

Though the railroad and Interurban were both reliable, they often did not take people where they wanted to go when they wanted to go there. The emergence of the automobile helped in this, but many roads were in such bad condition that they weren't practical for the auto. This resulted in continuing pressure on national, state and local governments to build more and better roads.

The Good Roads Movement, which was particularly embraced by farmers, was one prominent example of this trend. One of the cornerstones of the movement was the idea that the nation should have a coast-to-coast highway serving the southern part of the nation.

Senator John Hollis Bankhead of Alabama was instrumental in persuading Congress to approve such a highway, U.S. 80, via the Federal Aid Road Act of 1916. The highway would begin in Washington, D.C. and end in San Diego, Calif. Construction began in earnest in the 1920s and continued, often through Works Projects Administration funds, in the 1930, with large sections of highway being constructed of bricks.

Bankhead Highway

Quickly dubbed the Bankhead Highway, in Texas the route ran through Texarkana, Mount Vernon, Terrell, Dallas, Arlington, Fort Worth, Mineral Wells, Abilene, Midland, and El Paso. The Arlington stretch of U.S. 80 was Division Street (Originally State Highway 1), and what happened along Division was typical of Bankhead Highway development in communities everywhere. Commerce developed and Arlington's once-square geometric configuration began to take a linear form along Division Street. By the 1940s, U.S. 80 was complete and visitors traveling across the nation on it would at some point pass through Arlington, many of whom would stop to eat, buy gas, have their car repaired or stay in a local hotel. The Arlington Auto Aisle, a long stretch of new car dealerships, developed an identity as the place to purchase a new or used auto.

Traveling along a U.S. highway in urban areas like Arlington, even in an automobile, would not be a particularly speedy process. By the 1950s, an estimated 80 or more stoplights existed on U.S. 80 between Dallas and Fort Worth. The capacity of such a two-lane highway, though adequate from the 1920s through 1940s, soon began to be insufficient, particularly when auto ownership began booming after World War II. Passage of the Interstate Highway Act of 1956 would eventually result in much of U.S. 80 traffic being diverted to other more efficient, parallel roadways.

For Arlington, this process began in 1957 in the form of the Dallas / Fort Worth Turnpike, a traffic-light-free, high traffic alternative to U.S. 80. Though the Turnpike had been visualized as early as 1944 it was not until 1953 that the legislature created the Texas Turnpike Authority. Then, in 1955, it persuaded voters to endorse the paid road project, promising to remove the tolls when the highway was paid off. On Aug. 27, 1957, the highway was opened to traffic.

Though the paid road design of the Turnpike did not provide the frontage roads that often result in a bonanza of commercial and residential development, it is clear that without it Arlington would not have been able to attract such amenities as Six Flags Over Texas, the Great Southwest Industrial District or Six Flags Mall. Nor would it have had the accessibility necessary for a boom in single family and multi-family development that would soon make Arlington one of the fastest growing municipalities in America.

Bonds for the Turnpike were paid off well in advance of projections, and though the Turnpike Authority made a case that the tolls should remain, voters insisted that the promise of a free road be kept. The bonds were paid off at the end of 1977, at which point the 30-mile road was turned over to the state and toll collections ceased. Originally designated as part of Interstate 20, the roadway was redubbed I-30 when the current Interstate Highway 20 route in south Arlington began construction in 1971. In 2001 the former Turnpike was labeled as the Tom Landry Highway after legendary Dallas Cowboys coach Tom Landry. It remains the primary access to the city's ever-growing Entertainment District.

Every silver cloud has a dark lining, of course, and this was no different for I-30. Traffic on once-busy U.S. 80/Division Street shrank to a fraction of its former level. The new car component of the Arlington Auto Aisle disappeared, relocating to locations on or near either I-20 or I-30. Most long-time Arlington residents and visitors alike would agree that long stretches of Division Street now represent the city's most prominent urban eyesore, though the 2008 arrival of the Dallas Cowboys and resurging downtown area provide hope that redevelopment will gradually occur.

The Parks Mall

If the presence of I-30 proved to be a boom to Arlington, the construction of Interstate 20 that began in the early 1970s would prove to be an even more powerful incentive for development, contributing dramatically an essential element to the city's status as the fastest growing city in the nation during the 1980s. Arlington added more population than either Dallas or Fort Worth during the era, its proponents noting that the city was also growing faster than giant municipalities like Chicago and New York City.

Though members of the Arlington City Council originally created a master plan that visualized much of I-20 as a vast silicon city, high tech and office building corridor, market forces showed very little interest in this idea. Though the city was able to attract one such entity, National Semiconductor, but very little else of this genre showed up. Likewise a Las Colinas-style office park called The Highlands, located a few blocks east of the I-20/Cooper Street intersection, opened in 1987. The venture eventually failed and the development's centerpiece, a giant, five-acre cluster of granite carvings created by artist Norman Hines, was turned over to the city, eventually being moved to Richard Greene Linear Park adjacent to the Texas Rangers Ballpark and Cowboys Stadium.

The marketplace did, however, very much like the idea of retail, restaurants and auto dealerships along I-20 in Arlington. The Parks of Arlington Mall opened in 1987 and was an immediate success, as was retail development in the former Highlands business park. Auto dealerships—some of which had a history tracing back to the Arlington Auto Aisle on Division Street—quickly became state or national sales leaders. Key intersections along I-20, such as those at Cooper Street and Little Road, were for a time among the most highly prized commercial locations in the nation, attracting big box retailers like Wal-Mart, K-Mart and Target. The population center of Arlington began moving southward toward I-20 as residential construction boomed and the commuting pattern was aided by both I-20 and the completion of a vast loop around the city called Green Oaks Boulevard—itself a popular location for commercial development.

There was, of course, the usual downside. Neither Six Flags Mall, which opened in 1970, nor its competing mall Forum 303 opening in 1971, both located near S.H. 360—could compete with The Parks. Or with the eventual arrival of upscale competitor Arlington Highlands, that broke ground in fall 2005, promptly expanding past its original 600,000 square foot beginnings. Though Six Flags Mall continues to exist, its future viability remains in doubt. Forum 303, after failing at other venues, was demolished in 2005, to be replaced by a business park.

Dallas / Fort Worth International Airport

Though Arlington was not a partner in creating Dallas/Fort Worth International Airport, it has benefited from proximity to what is now the fourth busiest airport in the world, with access by auto typically being only 15 to 20 minutes away. The DFW airport was completed in 1973.

Access to transportation amenities has shaped Arlington's history and growth patterns and will continue to do so. If there's a missing component to the equation it would be mass transit. One of the oft-repeated oddities about Arlington's transportation history is that it is not only the most populous city in the nation without mass transit; it is the only municipality within the 100 largest cities that does not provide bus or rail transit or both.

This is not an accidental phenomenon. Voters looked at the issue on three occasions, the idea being to dedicate a portion of the city's sales tax share to either creating a local system or joining existing systems in Dallas or Fort Worth. Each of those three separate proposals were rejected by voters with margins so substantial that most local political leaders have decided advocacy has so much potential to anger the electorate that the preference is to avoid the topic. While voters have been quick to reject mass transportation funding, they have been more amenable to approving taxpayer support of amenities like the Rangers' ballpark and then the Cowboys' stadium—both of which are technically owned by the city. The dilemma in this is that monies that would otherwise be available for mass transit have been invested elsewhere, meaning that at this writing there are insufficient economic resources to fund local mass transit. The Legislature has also been historically reluctant to allow other types of funding, such as increasing the maximum sales tax rate. Meanwhile, Arlington voters repeatedly demonstrated that they will not approve new taxes for mass transit.

The "why not" of this is difficult to analyze, though critics of mass transit have historically made issues of both the deficits at which mass transit systems operate and that both the population density—the number of residents per square mile—and the dispersed employment patterns of auto-reliant, commuting workers do not lend themselves to a workable mass transit system. Put simply, this means the majority of voters do not want to pay for a service they probably will not use. Factors such as escalating fuel prices, air pollution issues and other auto costs may change mind sets over time, but it will require a combination of changes in conditions, an attitudinal shift and a more proactive leadership before Arlingtonites will embrace mass transit. Just as cities like Boston were shaped enormously by trolley and bus lines, auto reliance—and a mid-Metroplex location—shaped Arlington, a pattern that will not easily change.

Early Media

The definition of community implies a place where information and ideas are communicated and shared. Though radio, television and the Internet have made the world something of a global village, in an earlier era—for example 1883—the local newspaper would have served as the primary instrument of shared community information.

Arlington's first newspaper came into being in 1877, though The Arlington Banner quickly disappeared. The first newspaper with staying power showed up in1883, a year before the city would officially be incorporated as a legal state municipality. Its name was "The World," a grandiose title for a single broadsheet of paper printed on a Washington flat press in a shed near the railroad station, the paper serving a growing village of perhaps 500 people. Lumber yard owner Col. Thomas Spruance and Willis Timmerman established the paper, printed once weekly. Few copies remain, but The World, edited and run by Timmerman, seemed to exist with a few ads and notices, excerpts from newspapers and magazines dropped off by train passengers and whatever informational tidbits Timmerman picked up about town.

Timmerman liked to brag that Arlington's residents "could buy the world for only a dollar," that being the price of a year's subscription. The power to make people briefly famous made Timmerman a popular man, so much so that he was eventually elected mayor. Though many editors and publishers to come would have great influence, none other than Timmerman would be both editor of the paper and mayor of the town.

Timmerman changed the name of the paper to "The Arlington Democrat" in 1893, a change that reflected the paper's political philosophy and affiliation, also changing the publication date from Thursday to Saturday. W.W. Warlick became editor in 1894, though it is uncertain if Spruance and Timmerman were still owners. Another newspaper, the Arlington Argus, also was briefly present around 1892. It was an era in which anyone with access to a printing press and the ability to hand-set type could create a newspaper, with many small publications arriving and departing with little fanfare.

John McGraw of Dallas, a Republican, bought the Arlington Democrat in 1895. His political views were much in conflict with his predecessors and an editorial denouncing the free silver policy advocated by the highly popular William Jennnings Bryan brought a protest group of about 100 people—McCraw termed it "a mob"—to the paper. Bryan declined the group's invitation that he leave town, but sold the paper in 1897 to George Byus, who promptly lowered the subscription rate to 50 cents annually and renamed the paper "The Arlington Journal." Byus began adding the occasional photograph to the paper, many taken by the city's quasi-official photographer, A.J. Mahaney.

Charles Kent and Karl Word took over The Arlington Journal in 1899, incorporating the first ever gasoline engine in the city to power their press. In a few years the paper would also be the first local business to use electric power for commercial purposes.

The writing style of the late 1800s and early 1900s tended to be considerably more first-person than modern journalism's tell-both-sides dictates, and there was a clear tendency toward community boosterism. Well-known local figures were often referred to with last name only. Nor was there much use of direct quotations. Here's a sample of a 1901 Journal article about a shooting as written by Editor Word.

Sample of 1901 Journal Article

Our little city was thrown into a fever of excitement yesterday when it became known that a killing had taken place in the heart of town with the knowledge of but a few.

A reporter for the Journal was on the scene soon after the shooting occurred. The sight which met our gaze was calculated to make stout hearts grow faint.

Joseph W. Oldfield was lying on the floor in the rear of Johnson's restaurant breathing his last with a gunshot wound just behind the left ear.

Immediately after the killing J.M. Young surrendered to City Marshall Douglas and was locked up.

We called on Mr. Young and asked him if he wished to make any statement for publication but he declined, and so we were unable to secure the facts leading up to the killing..

Oldfield was shot while sitting at the lunch counter in Johnson's restaurant. He was shot from the sidewalk, the load passing through the screen door and entered his skull all in a lump

In the afternoon Tom Kilgore was arrested, and as Sheriff Clark arrived from Fort Worth at 11 a.m. he took them both to Fort Worth on the 2:25 train yesterday evening.

The deceased was about 25 years old, a school teacher and stood high in the community. He leaves a wife and child. Young, after the killing, expressed himself as satisfied that he would have no trouble in securing an acquittal, but refused to talk for publication. All parties connected with the tragedy stand well in the community.

The case is being investigated by the grand jury now in session, other witnesses are being examined today.

The funeral took place from the Baptist church at 1 o'clock and the remains were followed to the grave by a large number of friends.

Harry Johnson bought the paper in 1901, printing the occasional extra and adding content that included gifts to brides and expansive coverage of new business openings. In 1902 he sold The Arlington Journal to owners with greater staying power, Laten and William Stanberry—the first long-time proprietors of the local paper. On occasion the brothers disagreed with each other and wrote opposing editorials, though William was officially the editor and Laten the business manager. Though a strong prohibitionist, Editor Stanberry consistently took positions advocating limitations on African-American citizens and opposing women's suffrage. On the suffrage issue he wrote:

> Thousands of women today have
> their eyes turned in the wrong
> direction for happiness. They
> need not look towards the polls;
> it is not there; they need not look
> away from home, it is not there.

The paper, however, was a commercial success, often running as many as 12 pages. The brothers eventually took in a partner, John Nichols, and continued to update printing equipment, adding a Linotype for automated typesetting printed on a new Babcock press. Nichols in 1907 purchased outright ownership of the paper. He soon found the business not to his liking and in 1908 sold the paper to a future community legend, Col. William Bowen—namesake for Bowen Road in Arlington.

Bowen was 51 when he purchased The Arlington Journal and had a long history of newspaper experience. He understood the power of boosterism and his hallmark phrase "The Great Arlington Country" really represented the first attempt to brand the city. Bowen also started the Farmer's Fireside Bulletin, the official publication of the Farmers Co-operative Union in Texas at a time when agrarian interests dominated politics. His "Uncle Zeke's Speculations" was written in African-American dialect. Bowen died in 1921. His obituary characterized him as a "picturesque figure," a hero to the farmers' movement and warrior in the "crusade against John Barleycorn." But it was also clear that he regarded African-Americans as second class citizens.

Bowen's wife remained owner of the paper for several years, leasing it to a succession of editors, the paper finally falling into the hands of the Perry newspaper family in 1925. The leased ownership went to Luther Perry in 1929, who finally bought the paper outright from the Bowen family in 1931. Perry ran the paper until 1947, leasing it for two years to his sons-in-law, briefly running the paper again in 1949 until selling it in 1950 to Albert Altwegg and Dick Weicker, both from Illinois. The 1950 census fixed the Arlington population at about 7,800.

"Perry reported on the rise and fall of horse racing in Arlington, the destruction of many stills, the shortages and other hardships brought on by World War II, and the beginning of Arlington's rapid growth," wrote Phyllis Forehand in her 1977 master's degree thesis on the history of the Arlington Citizen-Journal. That thesis has become the definitive resources for early newspaper history in Arlington.

Altwegg and Weicker were looking for a city with growth potential and believed—correctly as it turned out—that they found it in Arlington. Both had newspaper experience and were really the first operators of The Arlington Journal to subscribe to conventional, modern newspaper values, an established "beat" system and more extensive use of photographs, not as easily done in the pre-offset press era. By 1955 the paper had gone to twice-weekly publication. They broke stories about General Motors coming to Arlington and the pending arrival of the Great Southwest Industrial District.

The Journal had no real competition until 1934 when self-dubbed "Country Editor" A.H. Wheeler published the first edition of the Arlington Citizen. Wheeler was happy to barter goods for advertising and he also ventured into radio, hosting "The Country Editor" first at radio KTAK, then the bigger KFJZ, mixing his commentaries with music from groups like the Hardie Family Circle Band and Quartet. Eventually the show ran six days a week and had sponsors like Safeway supermarkets. Political correctness was not yet in vogue and the show often included conversations between Wheeler and his "colored office boy, Sambo." Wheeler eventually ran, unsuccessfully, for congress. Though Wheeler for a time passed control of the paper to a son-in-law, he was running the publication when it was sold to yet another Arlington legend, George W. Hawkes, in 1946. Wheeler died in 1951.

Hawkes, a Flatonia, Texas, resident, started on newspapers as a printing assistant in high school but his gift for flowing literacy of unusual eloquence soon became evident. By the time he finished high school he was the Flatonia Argus's star reporter, eventually purchasing the paper before he was legally old enough to sign a contract. While working on a Nacogdoches newspaper Hawkes discovered that Wheeler wanted to sell The Arlington Citizen. Hawkes bought it, quickly discovering that the paper had only 200 paid subscribers. George brought in his brother Charles to help with what almost amounted to a new newspaper startup. The 16-page paper the pair produced the first week actually made a little money with the two selling ads, writing newspaper copy and taking photos. "We had to," George Hawkes said. "We had no capital."

Though the Hawkes were skilled and high volume journalists by weekly newspaper standards, they were not particularly aggressive as reporters, often aligning the paper editorially with city and school district leadership—particularly true during the era when Tom Vandergriff was mayor and James Martin was school district superintendent. Arlington was probably not big enough for two newspapers, but then a third entity arrived, the Arlington Daily News, printed offset when its two competitors were still using the less glossy hot-type process. Indeed, Daily News Texan Publisher Stanley McBrayer was considered one of the inventors of the offset newspaper press. Something had to give, so in 1957 the Hawkes bought The Arlington Journal, buying Altwegg's share outright and incorporating Weicker's share, Weicker becoming the new company's business manager. Though the Journal and Citizen continued to be published separately for a while on different days, they were finally merged into The Arlington Citizen-Journal, a combination that made the Arlington Daily News a minor player locally even after it was purchased by Belo Corp., owners of the Dallas Morning News.

The Belo purchase did, however, alarm Fort Worth Star-Telegram publisher Amon Carter, who in 1964 bought controlling interest in the Citizen-Journal, leaving Hawkes and Weicker as minority owners and operators. Infused with funding from the highly profitable Star-Telegram the Citizen-Journal opened a new, non-union offset printing plant at 500 E. Front Street in 1965. In 1971 it moved to a new state-of-the-art photo typesetting and offset building on West Abram Street. The end of the Hawkes era came shortly after the 1974 purchase of the Star-Telegram and its holdings by Capital Cities. The Hawkes' remaining interests were purchased by Capital Cities. The Hawkes brothers and Weicker departed, ending almost 30 years of continuous ownership. Though the Citizen-Journal struggled to make major profits, it dominated competitors with the Texas Press Association and North and East Texas Press Association and was consistently regarded as one of the best large weekly papers in the nation.

Capital Cities would eventually become Capital Cities/ABC TV, which would be purchased by Disney, which would spin off the newspapers from the purchase to Knight-Ridder, which eventually would sell all of its newspapers to McClatchy Newspapers. The Star-Telegram would begin emphasizing zoned advertising and news and—after distributing the Citizen-Journal in the Star-Telegram for a while— eventually replace the Arlington Citizen-Journal with the Arlington Star-Telegram. For a while the Star-Telegram and Dallas Morning News would battle for supremacy in Arlington, expending millions of dollars on zoned publications before the Morning News—having killed the Arlington Daily News—finally withdrew.

In 2010 the Star-Telegram resurrected the Citizen-Journal name, producing a small, tabloid insert on a weekly basis—a small vestige of the Arlington-dominant newspaper it once was. In 2010 the Star-Telegram sold its Arlington newspaper building on West Abram St. At this writing the future of many newspapers—as printed products on paper—remains in doubt. The rapidly emerging dominance of the Internet erodes and continues to damage the viability of ink on paper, as well as the status of newspapers as information gatekeepers. Nevertheless, the shared information of newspapers stretching back from 1877 to the present—the city's success, failures, changes and people— was critical to the evolution of modern-day Arlington.

Chapter 11 – Thirty-nine Significant Arlington Stories

The Bridge

Every town seems to have a bridge where some catastrophic accident happened, and in this Arlington is no different.

On the evening of Feb. 4, 1961, a car carrying six Arlington teenage girls plunged off a burned out wooden bridge along the Trinity River bottoms area on what was then Arlington-Bedford Road (the road has since been rerouted and designated Greenbelt Road). In what appeared to be a prank gone badly wrong, barricades and signage closing the bridge had been removed. Three of the girls in the car died when their vehicle crashed into the other side of the ravine. The other three were seriously injured.

The bridge that now exists is actually a couple of hundred yards west of the former wooden bridge. Though several young men were eventually charged with removing the barricades, it remains unclear who set the fire that originally damaged the bridge.

Allan Saxe

Few Arlington residents have been as philanthropic as UT Arlington political science professor, author, humorist and TV commentator Allan Saxe.

Saxe joined the UTA faculty in 1965. Frugal in lifestyle by nature, Saxe—who in demeanor and appearance has a Woody Allen persona—began acquiring paintings by noted artists such as Picasso, often buying the works much as one might purchase an auto via monthly payments. Fretful by inclination, Saxe worried so much about the security of his art investment that he began donating the paintings to institutes like the university and city.

He candidly admitted that he enjoyed the attention and began making cash donations to a multitude of causes, from short-term loan programs to students and "Allen Saxe pencil sharpeners" to more expansive donations, the funds for which were from either his professorial earnings or inheritance. The result was that his name appears on foyers, lobbies, mezzanines, hospitals, animal shelters, sports facilities and even the Allan Saxe Road to the Landfill.

He also was an unsuccessful candidate for Arlington City Council despite what may have been the most popular local campaign bumper sticker in the city's history. Thousands of students altered his "Saxe for Arlington" sticker, cutting out the "e" in his name and sticking it over the "a," resulting in several years of "Sex for Arlington" bumper stickers.

Allan Saxe also is the author of "Politics of Arlington, Texas."

Tillie Burgin

Mission Arlington and Mission Metroplex creator, Tillie Burgin, has often been labeled as the "Mother Teresa of Arlington" for good reason. Once a missionary for a decade in Korea, Burgin found herself asking this question: "If we could do missions in Korea, why can't we do missions in Arlington?" In 1986 she and others began Mission Arlington with the goal of meeting the needs of less fortunate people through Bible studies, medical and dental services, child and adult day care, clothing, food, furniture, transportation and counseling. The program boomed, expanding to Mission Metroplex in 1990. Both Burgin and Mission Arlington/Mission Metroplex have won acclaim as an example of altruistic social services provided by the religious sector, including presidential recognition of the missions as a national "Point of Light."

Miracle Lake

Lake Arlington might have begun as "Vandergriff's Folly" but it was quickly redesignated "Miracle Lake." Though the arrival of General Motors in the early 1950s certainly heralded a future of growth for the city, it also created a problem for then-Mayor Tom Vandergriff: An expanding GM plant would soon utilize all the water the city's well system could produce. Vandergriff's answer was to build the 2,250-acre Lake Arlington in the Village Creek watershed. Opponents of the plan labeled the idea as "Vandergriff's folly" and said the lake would take years to fill. Built for slightly more than $3.8 million, impoundment took place on March 31, 1957. It began raining almost right away, rain that returned every day for 27 consecutive days in what still remains as one of the wettest months in history for this region. The lake filled before April 1957 ended. Though an urban myth persists that the lake filled so rapidly that construction equipment like bulldozers had to be abandoned, this is not accurate, though a bridge at the south end of the reservoir had to be dynamited after the lake filled. The lake also overflowed the site of the original Lake Erie Pavilion, a once-popular recreation spot on a large pond on what is now the northwest side of the lake near the Handley Interurban stop. The Tarrant Water District now pumps additional water into the lake from East Texas reservoirs.

Berachah Home

The Berachah Home was established in Arlington on May 14, 1903, by the Rev. J. T. Upchurch and his wife, Maggie Mae, as the Berachah Industrial Home for the Redemption of Erring Girls. It operated under various names as an establishment for homeless, usually pregnant girls, in part by the Berachah Society in Dallas as part of the Nazarene Church.

The home closed in 1935, but was reopened later that year by the Upchurch's daughter, Allie Mae, and her husband, Frank Wiese, as the Berachah Child Institute. The Institute ceased operation in 1942. The University of Texas at Arlington purchased the property—west of Cooper and Mitchell streets—in 1963.

The home's official papers are now part of Special Collections on the sixth floor of the university library. A small cemetery west of Davis Hall is all that remains of the home.

No Drinkin', No Dancin'

Arlington had three saloons when voters voted in favor of municipal prohibition in 1902. For a while this provision was skirted via creation of "dance halls" that were somewhat saloon-like. Voters took care of this loophole in 1905 by also prohibiting dance halls. The Arlington Journal editorialized about the closing, noting "Of all the blots on the fair name of Texas, few are darker than the dance hall. They come nearer being an excuse for an open saloon; the gambling hall is more respectable and not productive of half the evil and evil influences."

First United Methodist Church

The First United Methodist Church began its existence in 1878 after several residents met in the offices of Shultz Lumber Yard at the corner of Front and Mesquite streets, the business serving as the church meeting space for seven years. The church purchased property at the corner of Division and Center streets in 1884, building a frame structure that was replaced by a brick building in 1907. The church was destroyed or damaged by fires in 1918 and 1954, each time the church rebuilding. A sprawling church campus now occupies the original 1884 area, plus several acres acquired through purchases or contributions. Membership now exceeds 5,000.

The Tax Man

The Tax Man will always be around, though the collection methods may differ. Arlington's first funding method, created in 1884, was an annual occupational tax that varied by profession. Traveling salesmen and fortune tellers paid the highest tax, $87.50 (Local merchants did not like competition while fortune tellers were likened to undesirable gypsies). Whiskey salesmen were charged $10 to $50. Clairvoyants, land agents, lawyers, dentists, food peddlers, cotton buyers and grain dealers—all apparently considered more desirable occupations—paid $2.50 yearly. A 1907 ordinance added a 50 cent dog tax, though the provision was considered a way to persuade farmers to not allow their sometimes troublesome dogs to come to town with them.

Arlington Public Library System

The Arlington Public Library System began in 1923 in a corner of the First National Bank lobby, moving to a small room in City Hall in 1928. The library was run by volunteers until the city took over the function in 1954. For many years the library operated out of the Cooper House at Meadowbrook Park.

Four Firsts

Though Arlington had an unofficial mayor before incorporation, the first mayor following 1884 incorporation was George Finger. Arlington politics favored males and Caucasians for decades, though voter inclinations have changed as the town's demographics steadily reflected less gender and racial bias. It wasn't until 1972 that the first woman served on the council, with UT Arlington urban studies graduate student and banker Martha Walker unseating an incumbent to gain that distinction. Arlington residents elected the council's first Hispanic, Dan Serna, a CPA, and its first African American, retired postal inspector Elzie Odom, in 1990. Odom later became the city's first African American mayor.

Plant Owner A.W. Collins

It seemed wasteful to corn-shelling plant owner A.W. Collins to simply burn corn cobs, and in 1904 he began using the cobs as fuel for the first electric generation system in Arlington. Electricity was available only for lighting and customers paid a set monthly fee depending on how many light bulbs they lit. Collins mixed lignite coal with other refuse when his cob and shuck supply ran low. Power was initially available from dusk until 11 p.m. weekdays and until midnight Saturdays. The plant was expanded in 1906, providing 220 volts of direct current. Full time service wasn't available until 1913 when the electrical system was bought out by the North Texas Traction Company, the Interurban operators. The company replaced the direct current system with more efficient alternating current at 115 volts. The first commercial user of electricity was Arlington Journal Publisher William Bowen, who used an electric motor to power his press.

First Baptist Church

Put a few Baptists together and pretty soon there'll be a church. Arlington's booming First Baptist Church began in 1876 at Johnson Station, though not much is known of that early history since a 1911 fire destroyed much of the church's early documents.

When the Texas and Pacific Railroad came through a few miles north, the little group of Baptists moved their church there as well in a small frame building at Oak and Border streets. The church briefly disbanded after 1900 but re-formed in 1916 with 21 members, calling themselves Arlington Baptist Church until 1941 when the name was changed to First Baptist. A 1944 fire destroyed the church building at Abram and Pecan streets. With more than 5,000 members the church now occupies several city blocks in downtown Arlington.

First Presbyterian Church

The First Presbyterian Church of Arlington began in 1888 as a subset of Cumberland Presbyterian Church, the first organizing minister being D.G. Malloy. From 1893 until 1956 the church was located on Abram Street near Pecan Street. The church outgrew its facilities and moved to 1200 South Collins Street in 1956.

Harlington

Arlington would probably be Harlington were it not for an error by the clergy scribe who left out the "H" in a royal appointment of Henry Bennett as the 1st Earl of Arlington, an offshoot of his peerage as Baron Arlington of Harlington. The clergy considered such typographical nuances to be God's will and rarely changed them. Arlington, Va., was named in the earl's honor, subsequent Arlingtons following the same pattern. Harlington is now a suburb of London.

The control of foreign affairs was entrusted to the earl. One of his duties as keeper of the privy purse (financial manager of the royal household) was to procure and manage the royal mistresses.

Abram Street

It's likely that the most oft mispronounced roadway in Arlington is Abram Street, which is frequently referred to as "Abrams" with an "s," even by many long-time Arlington residents.

The source of the name may either be W.W. Abrams, a land commissioner who dispensed titles along the wagon road that would become Abram, or Abraham (aka Abe or Abram) Harris, a pioneer resident.

Regardless, Abram was once State Highway 1 but became U.S. 80. As Highway 1, Abram—for years called Dallas-Fort Worth Road or "The Pike"—was the city's main drag until U.S. 80 was authorized. Highway builders decided it would be more cost efficient to have 80 on the north side of the railroad track, which in Arlington would be a dirt road called Division Street. This decision would also avoid incorporating "Death's Crossing" into U.S. 80. Abram ended at present-day Fielder Road and took a 90-degree turn north across both the Interurban and T&P railroad tracks, a hazardous and sometimes fatal combination. Arlington officials protested the route change, preferring to keep highway traffic on Abram or Main streets. When offered an option of either paying for the highway themselves or accepting the Division Street alternative, they allowed the route change, albeit not happily. A tunnel—now closed—was built under the new highway to allow elderly residents of the Masonic Home to cross safely.

The Marshal

One of Arlington's most beloved figures was "the marshal," a smallish, intellectually challenged and likeable man named Marshall Morton, long since deceased. A Texas Monthly article once described Morton as "gnome like." Marshall, often wearing cap pistols, took his first name seriously, sometimes directing traffic stopped for a passing train. He often participated in Arlington High School and Arlington State College halftime ceremonies and frequented all Western movies at the two downtown theaters, typically offering cautions to cowboys heroes like Hopalong Cassidy or "Lash" LaRue along the lines of, "Watch out Hoppy! He's right behind you!" The community essentially adopted Morton as a beloved eccentric.

Arlington Crystals

You can take a horse to water, but sometimes you can't make him drink. That's particularly true if the water is heavily mineralized, as was the mineral well that Arlington drilled in the middle of Main and Center streets in 1891. The well had so much natural pressure that for around 20 years the water flowed to the surface and ran down Center Street.

Though the original intent had been to provide drinking water, Arlington tried to make the most of the situation by promoting itself as a mineral water resort city. The city eventually licensed Gilbert Y. Luke and his brothers, R.S. and Paul, to use the water for the Epson-salt-like

Arlington Crystals at a rate of a ton a day. The Lukes connected a pipeline from the well to their building in the 200 block of E. South Street, utilizing 16 gallons of water for every pound of crystals.

The crystal business eventually declined. The well was capped in 1951, declared a traffic hazard and cleared from Main and Center in 1972, though a wellhead still exists under Center Street. The Lukes eventually became Pontiac and Honda dealers.

Arlington GM Plant

The original plan for the Arlington GM plant was that it would produce both cars and Gruman aircraft. Construction of the plant was already underway in 1952 when the Navy cancelled the aircraft project. The plant had been possible through the marketing efforts of 25-year-old "Boy Mayor" Tom Vandergriff and his father, Chevrolet and Buick dealership owner W.T. "Hooker" Vandergriff.

Working as unpaid agents for GM, the two put together several plots of land for the 250 acres needed, including a church campground and acreage owned by upcoming electronics magnate Curtis Mathes. The first car, a black Pontiac Chieftain, rolled off the assembly line in January 1954. It took 10 years for the millionth car to be assembled but only six more for the two millionth, an Oldsmobile Cutlass.

The plant almost closed in the early 1990s but an expanded blitz by then Mayor Richard Greene—with multi-governmental and union collaboration—produced an assortment of incentives that persuaded GM to retain its Arlington plant while closing others. It is currently the only SUV producer for the big auto maker.

George Curtis Mathes

Scottish American George Curtis Mathes, the organizer of the TV-manufacturing Curtis Mathes Corp., called Arlington home. The company was created in 1957, eventually doing most of its manufacturing in a giant facility at Athens, Texas.

Mathes also had extensive land investments in Arlington, including the present-day sites of the Parks of Arlington and the Arlington

Highlands, the latter developed by his descendants. The Mathes family had a history of cabinet manufacturing, and its TVs were as much furniture as entertainment. The TV sets were advertised as the most expensive on the market "but darn well worth it."

The company went into a precipitous decline after Mathes was killed in a fire aboard a 1983 Air Canada flight. When the company was sold in 1988 it was the last remaining fully U.S. owned TV manufacturing company.

William Wright

Bedford preacher William Wright drove his horse and buggy to Arlington in 1881. The traveling evangelist held a sermon in the village school house, the first meeting of what would become First Christian Church (Disciples of Christ).

Two years later the congregation purchased two lots on South Street from the Texas and Pacific Railroad. The first church occupied the first floor and the Masonic Lodge the second. That church was eventually replaced with an Abram Street location, and in the 1950s the church moved to its current site on South Collins Street, expanding several times. Membership now exceeds 1,000.

Randol Mill Road

It's difficult to spend any time at all in Arlington without somehow ending up on Randol Mill Road, though doing so raises a question: Where's the mill that gives the road a name? The site of the actual Randol Mill is located in Fort Worth a hundred yards upstream from the Trinity River bridge on Precinct Line Road just off Randol Mill Road. Only a small vestige of the original grist mill dam remains.

R.A. Randol bought the mill site and rebuilt the mill in the 1880s. Over the course of its history, four men were killed during mill operations, which ceased in 1922. The mill area and building was a favorite site for picnickers and hobos, but the building burned in 1933 when apparently someone built a fire inside the building. An alleged "hanging tree" has long since been destroyed by lightning. Randol Mill

Park in Arlington has no connection to the mill other than adjoining the street. The 145-acre park was originally purchased for a public golf course but voters in 1954 turned that idea down by a scant two votes.

Arlington's First Post Office

According to the National Archives and Records Service, Arlington's first post office was located in the long-gone village of Hayter a couple of miles east of current downtown Arlington, and was established on July 29, 1875.

After the arrival of the railroad the post office was moved to Arlington on Jan. 22, 1877, with S.A. Daniel as the first postmaster. James Ditto became the city's second postmaster on July 30, 1877. In that era, local residents often served terms as postmaster, typically operating out of a corner of their stores.

The list of early postmasters includes a number of prominent pioneer residents, including Thomas Spruance, James Hammack, Benjamin Mathers and Carter Junior High namesake James Carter.

Arlington Rotary Club

The dean of Arlington Service Clubs is the Arlington Rotary Club, often referred to as "Downtown Rotary." The club was organized in May of 1923 with 17 members and Sam Wine as the first president. The 1923 members represented the elite of the business community, members in addition to Wine including Elvis Altman, Garner Ammon, Cliff Barnes, H.E. Cannon, Paul Chancellor, W.E. Clark, Leslie Coulter, Tom Cravens, Frank Hall, Gordon Hill, Ed McKnight, Hugh Moore, Thomas Spruance, Elmer Taylor and Myron Williams.

The club has been extraordinarily philanthropic and generous over the years, providing scholarships and ongoing contributions to a long list of causes: wheel chairs, polio immunizations and drilling water wells, funding foreign student exchange programs, and other scholarships, recognizing outstanding teachers and police and guaranteeing college scholarships to Webb Elementary students who eventually graduate from high school.

The Arlington Lion's Club

Chartered in January of 1942, is the second oldest service club in the city. The club has long been involved in support of youth, but has been particularly noted over the years for its involvement with providing eyeglasses for needy individuals.

Junior League of Arlington

No organization in Arlington has been more active in the area of women's concerns and children's issues than The Junior League of Arlington. Forty-four founding members created the League in July of 1975 with Pat Ellington as the first president. The idea was to promote volunteerism—every member is expected to participate in a community betterment assignment—and to demonstrate the effectiveness of trained volunteers.

The League also provides grants and funding for a variety of projects. Recent examples include support of the Smart Hospital in UT Arlington's nursing program, a Boys and Girls Club eight-week program promoting healthy lifestyle choices for at-risk girls and a unique AIDS outreach program for children that are either HIV positive or live with a family member who is HIV positive.

Social services agencies can request volunteers and also funding for long-term projects, short term community assistance and emergency needs.

Arlington's Unsolved Murders

Arlington has two famous unsolved murders that attracted national attention.

The first involved Cheryl Ann Callaway, 18, who was attacked by an unknown assailant when she left Forum 303 Mall on Jan. 30, 1974. Callaway was stabbed repeatedly with a weapon that police believed to be either an ice pick or awl-like tool. Some of the attack by an unidentified man was viewed by witnesses who also obtained a partial license plate from the vehicle he drove away.

No arrest, however, was ever made and no motivation for what appeared to be a random homicide was ever determined.

The second murder involved the Jan. 13, 1996, abduction of 9-year-old Amber Haggerman from the lot of an abandoned grocery store on East Abram Street. Amber pedaled her bicycle there from her grandparent's nearby house. A child witness said she was taken by a man driving a black pickup.

Four days later a man walking his dog found Amber's body in a North Arlington creek bed off Green Oaks Road. Her assailant was never found, but Amber's death resulted in the implementation of national AMBER Alert legislation, which has since resulted in the recovery of several kidnapped children.

City of Arlington Charter

The Bible for operation of a city is its charter, a sort of rules of order that determines the governing structure and boundaries of a municipality. The charter cannot be changed without approval of voters. Arlington operated as a simple village with a set of legal ordinances until voters approved a formal charter in 1920. A Charter Commission chaired by J.I. Carter wrote the original charter, the city's mayor at the time being W.H. Rose.

The charter established Arlington as a "home rule" city, which gave it the authority to create any ordinances not in conflict with state or national law. The original charter established a mayor who would serve as chief magistrate—in effect also the city manager—and four commissioners. Typically, each commissioner was assigned a critical component of municipal services to oversee. Arlington essentially maintained this style of governance until it adopted a city manager format in the late 1940s. Council members were elected at-large—representing the entire city—until a mixed format of single member and at-large members (nine in all counting the mayor) was adopted in 1993.

The mayor and commissioners under the 1920 charter were paid $10 a month. Today's council members are still essentially volunteers who are paid $200 a month, the mayor receiving $250.

Technological Progress

Progress, particularly of the technological sort, sometimes arrives in a hurry. Arlington began receiving not only expanded electrical service in 1906, but also the first telephones became available in homes and businesses through the predecessor to the Southwestern Telephone Service. The phone company implemented its first rate increase in 1908, to $2 per household, resulting in the first but not last city utility rate increase protest.

Also in 1908 the city decided that the existing privy and septic tank systems were simply not appropriate for a growing community and that a sewer system should be created. Arlington commissioner (councilman) J.P Fielder took the lead in studying and creating the city's first sewage treatment plant based on a Brownwood design. The first treatment plant was located on Johnson Creek in what is now the southwest corner of Meadowbrook Park.

Crystal Canyon Gold

One of the most popular fantasies of pioneer residents was that they would be the one to find the "Crystal Canyon Gold." In 1856 an Army mule train was attacked by Indians as it approached the Bird's Fort area near the Trinity River in North Arlington. The train was carrying 10 bars of gold. All but two of the Indians were killed, but one of them, though possibly wounded, escaped with the gold. He traveled through a ravine in north Arlington—describing it as a canyon may be overly descriptive—that is littered with odd crystal deposits. The belief was that the Indian buried the heavy ingots in the area because it was hindering his escape.

No gold was ever found, or at least never found and reported. Crystal Canyon—located near Green Oaks Boulevard east of Collins Street — was once slated to be developed for apartments but now is city park property.

Christmas Eve Shootout

Arlington does not have the old west reputation of Fort Worth, but it did have a legendary Christmas Eve shootout in 1892. The actual fight took place on Dec. 23, but showed up in papers on Christmas Eve.

A dispute over livestock between J.H. Hargrove of Bowie and Harvey Spears of Arlington resulted in Hargrove bringing his sons George and Walker on the train to Arlington, where they were met by Spears and his friend "Poker" Bill Smith. A six-shooter emptying, depot shootout resulted in which the only survivor was Walker Hargrove, who subsequently was found to have acted in self-defense.

A stranger riding through town had his horse accidentally shot out from under him, and residents took up a collection to buy a new horse. Walker Hargrove was eventually killed in a saloon gunfight.

Zack Bobo

There has always been an abundance of doctors in Arlington since the first physicians settled in the area in the 1880s, such as Dr. J.D. Collins, who built the privately-owned Arlington Sanitarium.

But the physician most associated with Arlington since the 1950s is Dr. Zack Bobo, who originally operated out of a giant old ranch house that he had converted into a mini-hospital, on Center St across from the First Baptist Church. Bobo was also a quiet philanthropist, in particular funding hundreds of scholarships to Baylor University.

International Bowling Museum Hall of Fame

Arlington became the equivalent to the world bowling center when the International Bowling Museum and Hall of Fame moved to the city's Entertainment District in 2010.

Bowling, in its various forms, has a history stretching back 50 centuries, which the museum displays. The facility has its own bowling lanes that are used for both testing of new products and exhibitions. The building is also headquarters for bowling's Team USA and Junior Team USA, as well as other bowling-associated organizations.

Hurricane Harbor

Hurricane Harbor opened originally as the $18.5 million Wet 'n Wild Park, which made its debut in spring of 1982. Six Flags purchased Wet 'n Wild in 1995, changing the name to Hurricane Harbor in 1997, the change reflecting a new Caribbean theme.

The Hill

The centerpiece for Arlington's largest African American neighborhood, dubbed "The Hill," was Mount Olive Baptist Church, established in 1897.

A large wooden structure housing the church was built in 1912 at the northern dead end of West Street, the building also serving as the African American Masonic Lodge. The church is now located on Sanford Street.

Football Champs

In Texas, it is difficult to win a state championship in football. The sole local state champion was the Arlington High School Colts team of 1951. The school's all-state fullback, Cecil "Rusty" Gunn, made the game's only touchdown, but that was enough for a win over Waco La Vega for the state 2A title.

Arlington has a long fascination with football, the first formal playing of the game taking place in 1904 between Carlisle Academy (now UTA) and Oak Cliff.

Shut the Ponies Down

Though Arlington Downs and horse racing were a financial success in Arlington, Bible Belt opposition to pari-mutuel betting was a frequent pulpit discussion item.

Ministers like J. Frank Norris and the Rev. W.T. Rouse of Arlington Baptist Church strongly opposed the presence of the track. Church groups found a sympathetic ear in Gov. James Allred and in 1937 the Legislature repealed pari-mutuel betting.

The track continued to host events like auto racing and rodeos for many years, also serving as a location for a movie called "To Please a Lady," filmed in 1950 and starring Clark Gable and Barbara Stanwyck.

In 1958, Arlington Downs was flattened to make room for the Great Southwest Industrial District, though a portion of the grandstand was transported to a race track in New Mexico, also since demolished.

The Magic Middle

Though Arlington residents today generally consider train traffic through the middle of the city to be a traffic-stopping nuisance, the community owes its very existence to the Texas and Pacific Railroad's decision to create a stop midway between Dallas and Fort Worth.

For many years the Texas and Pacific Depot at Center and Main streets was the heart of the city's transportation and shipping activity, additionally providing passenger rail service for many years. The depot, which was torn down in 1952, also was the site of a now-famed 1892 gunfight that left four men dead. The city in later years was given an option to create an Amtrak stop in the city but would have had to finance its own depot. The city declined to make the investment.

Masonic Retirement Center in Arlington

The Mason's Grand Royal Arch Chapter opened the Texas Masonic Retirement Center in Arlington in 1911 on a hundred acres, some of which was eventually sold for an apartment complex when Fielder Road was extended north and cut off a section of the estate.

Originally the home also grew some of its own cattle and other food and included a hospital, since demolished. A tunnel under U.S. 80 (now closed) connected the center to the local Masonic chapter on Abram Street.

The Eastern Star Home was built in 1924 as a senior home for women members of the Masonic-related Eastern Star. Its residents were moved to the Masonic Home when the facility, located just south of the Cowboys stadium, was closed.

Number Please

By the time Arlington's first local telephone switchboard was opened in 1911 by Southwestern Bell, 300 customers had already signed up. The first manager was Henry Williamson, who initially hired boys to be switchboard operators. But customers found the youths to be sloppy, impatient and sometimes rude. Williamson began hiring young women as operators and service immediately improved.

Keep It Under 10 MPH

The growing presence of automobiles in the early part of the 20th century made it necessary for the city to establish its first speed limit in 1911. Vehicles could drive no faster than 10 mph.

Police either walked or used horses until 1912 when the city purchased its first motorized law enforcement vehicles—motorcycles, then costing $290 each.

Smart Mayor

Though many businesses in pre-1930 Arlington had secretaries, these generally were men, women rarely working outside the home. This precedent was believed to have been broken locally when Will Rose in 1911 hired the city's first woman secretary, Floy Brooks, to attend to clerical matters in his real estate business. Rose was eventually elected as the city's mayor.

Chapter 12 – Arlington Woman's Club

Arlington Woman's Club

The Arlington Woman's Club building on historic West Abram Street stands as more than an attractive blend of modern and Old South architecture, though it is both those things. It's also a symbol of Texas pluck, the power of community spirit, a stick-to-it resolve that has lasted for more than half a century and a presence that promises to be around for decades to come. In Texas parlance, the history of the Arlington Woman's Club makes for a good story. It is a tale of perseverance, dedication to community and a validation of the premise that people working together can make their community a better place. And it is also yet another example of a universal truism: Never underestimate the power of women with their minds made up.

Like most stories, it is best to start at the beginning. Though the formal creation of the Arlington Woman's Club did not occur until 1957, the roots of the organization go much further back, indeed to the 1930s and 1940s. Those roots had names like The Shakespeare Club (the oldest club in Arlington), the Arlington Music Club, the Arlington Garden Club, the Business and Professional Women's Club, The Roundabout Club (faculty wives at Arlington State College) and the Epsilon Sigma Alpha Club. Arlington then was a much smaller, almost rural place with just a few thousand residents and for the most part the members of the various women-oriented clubs knew each other, had shared interests and crossover membership was common.

But there was already something of a problem. The various civic groups had outgrown the ability to meet in members' homes and there was a shortage of public meeting spaces. The town was growing and the various clubs were growing with it.

"After the war in the 1940s the men came home, they all went to college and came out looking for jobs," recollects long-time Woman's Club member and former club President Jo Johnston. "And Arlington, this sleepy little farm town, had all these 'foreigners' arriving. We were known as that because we were not kin to anybody in town. But little by little the people on the block began to invite us to join them at the Club Center of Arlington and we became involved."

The Club Center was born in May of 1950. A group of women representing the aforementioned clubs of Arlington met with then-Mayor B.C. Barnes and other council officials to discuss the possibility of the various city clubs using the City Hall auditorium for meetings. Arlington by then had a population of just 7,800. Berta Brown represented the clubs and made an eloquent appeal. City officials were amenable to the suggestion but wanted something in return, that being a spiffed up auditorium. Brown outlined the need for such a place and told the council the clubs would do all the cleaning, painting and refurbishing as the auditorium was in poor condition and the city had its customary shortage of funds. Barnes and the council agreed and the women wasted no time getting the ball rolling, renaming the auditorium as Club Center and electing Brown as the first president.

"A series of money-making plans were made post haste," long-time member Dorothy Rencurrel said. "The first was a barbeque held at Arlington's then-only park, Meadowbrook. Hooker Vandergriff's dealership lent the women pickup trucks to clean the park for the event. It was a financial success and the money was put into the treasury to buy paint for the Club Center. Shortly after that, the first gift to the Center was donated – an electric range from Texas Electric."

Other money-making events followed, some small and some larger: book review socials, pyramid luncheons and hot dog suppers. The proceeds from these enabled their first purchase – an electric refrigerator. And a new tradition began of members donating furnishings, one of the first being a large coffee urn provided by Misses Myrtle and Grace Thornton.

"Pretty soon they were able to buy a few card tables for the center instead of bringing their own," Rencurrel said.

All that activity and energy began attracting media attention. Al Altwegg, co-owner of The Arlington Journal, noted in his newspaper in 1951 that "One of the busiest places in town is the Woman's Club Center (one of the first 'Woman's Club' references) in the City Hall. Obviously the Center has filled a long-needed void in the community. One of the real accomplishments during the past year was the cleaning up, repainting and general refurbishing of the old auditorium to make it a Woman's Club Center."

In 1950, however, it would have been difficult for even the most optimistic community official to know what kind of population explosion was about to occur in Arlington. By 1957, the city had grown from its modest 7,800 residents to 34,000 – almost a five-fold increase – and new development was replacing what months before had been cotton and wheat fields. The boom was on and the city needed all the space it could get, including the old auditorium. The Club Center, by then more commonly called the Woman's Club Center, would have to vacate the premises.

It would have been easy enough and certainly forgivable if the women in the Club Center had simply decided to shrug and move on. But they did not. Woman's Club member Ethel Reeder recollects that the women who had been meeting at the Club Center were determined to secure a permanent home.

"So they held a Ten Dollar Tea in which they challenged the women to pay dues to a non-existent organization as a way to save toward their goal," Reeder said. "Sixty women paid $10 and this was the beginning of the Arlington Woman's Club Building Fund. The money was deposited in the bank and dues continued to pour in. The year (1957) ended with 232 paid members. And the fundraising continued full steam."

Not content with simply donating money, members had all kinds of fundraisers, raising a dollar here, $10 there. Sometimes a rummage sale was held, at which anything loose was up for sale.

"Marguerite Watson took off her shoes from Neiman's because her feet hurt, and somebody sold them for $2," Reeder said with a laugh. "There were also potluck suppers with members bringing their own food and paying 50 cents to eat it."

The new "Woman's Club," homeless though it was, had its first public meeting, a banquet in December of 1957 in the cafeteria of what was then Arlington State College, now the University of Texas at Arlington. Some 250 attended with Mayor Tom Vandergriff bringing the city's official blessing to the AWC new home project and the leaders of the Fort Worth Woman's Club also providing support. The first officers of the new organization were also elected at the event: President Ruth Grundy, Vice Presidents Mrs. W.T. Martin and Mrs. Earl Snowdon, Recording Secretary Mrs. Fred Hodges, Corresponding Secretary Mrs. M.W. Waldridge, Treasurer Mrs. Joe Rape and Parliamentarian Mrs. C.E. Collett. Members held meetings at their residences and other places while continuing to look for a permanent home.

An answer to the permanent home problem also turned out to be the answer to a city problem. The Arlington Library was housed in the historic Cooper House, a circa 1848 structure of Southern colonial antebellum architecture, but the building was of all-wood construction and no longer met fire codes requirements. Further, the weight of library stacks was too much for the house to sustain. When the city was forced to abandon the Cooper House in 1962, Woman's Club members seized upon the opportunity and petitioned the city council lease the home to the club. The council agreed but with a proviso: maintenance and care of the Cooper House would be the Woman's Club responsibility. Club members agreed, moving into the Cooper House at Meadowbrook Park in 1973.

"We spent the next few years refurbishing and furnishing it," Jo Johnston said. "Then when Marjorie Wilemon became president, we added the Cooper Room, which brought a new dimension because we could have meetings with more than 200 people."

Wilemon, a major figure in the club's history, was also the primary creator of a Woman's Club subset: the service-to-community oriented Junior Woman's Club, created in 1967 and generally considered the forerunner of the Junior League of Arlington. The first president was Stevie Campbell Hanson, daughter of AWC member Connie Campbell.

"The two clubs would work in different areas," former President Jo Johnston said. "The Junior Woman's Club would become involved in an incredible amount of both fund raising and hours contributed to other nonprofits. It was very much an on-going giving of themselves."

In Junior Woman's Club, every member had to serve on a committee and participate in philanthropy. Over the years they produced a yearly calendar, a cookbook and events like a tour of homes and Kaleidoscope, an original musical with talent from the community as well as members. The club initiated the Crest Award, designed with the Arlington Woman's Club seal, to recognize outstanding community service. Sue Stevens Durbec, chairwoman of the Community Study and Service Department, received the first Crest Award.

The Junior Woman's Club was phased out in 2000, the heir-apparent being the Junior League of Arlington. Philanthropy has always been a critical component of the Arlington Woman's Club, the objective of the organization being to both promote and develop the potential of its members through education and to benefit the community through philanthropic projects. AWC members, as individuals, give many thousands of hours to community services. The club itself also

contributes to nonprofits and provides scholarships. Some of the
organizations receiving AWC funds or other assistance over the years
include Arlington Urban Ministries, Miracle League of DFW, Mission
Arlington, Salvation Army, Family Life Center, Arlington Charities,
Meals on Wheels, Arlington Life Shelter, Christmas Samaritans, Safe
Haven, Families in Transition, Arlington Life Shelter, Grace After Fire,
and HOPE Tutoring, among others.

By 1998 the Cooper House was both a money pit – an investment
that club members were happy to make – and a national architectural
treasure when tragedy struck. What began as a 1998 Halloween night
prank went terribly wrong and the house was destroyed by fire. Arlington
firefighters were able to salvage most of the club's furnishings, a notable
accomplishment because many of the furnishings were valuable antiques
donated by members. But the fire created a familiar dilemma for the
AWC: The organization was once again homeless, but experience is a
good teacher. Club leadership knew that the club was now Phoenix-like,
always able to resurrect itself after a setback.

Vicki King, a former president of both the Junior Woman's Club
and eventually the Woman's Club itself, was appointed as the chairman
and one of seven Recovery Committee members to decide what AWC
was going to do after the fire. Others were Mary Lou Humphries, Sabre
Ellis, Lucy Thompson, Helen Bailey and Shirley Cole.

"Recovery Committee members didn't know where our future was
because we were essentially homeless organizations," King said. "But
we began looking. And looking. Before it was over we considered 28
pieces of property." King said as the search continued a theme
developed. Most existing buildings required too many renovations and
lacked a central location that would be accessible to all members.
Increasingly it looked as if new construction would be the best solution,
albeit with a problem: How to pay for it. Eventually the club settled on
almost two acres at 1515 W. Abram St., purchasing the land from the
adjoining Masonic organization.

"We had a wish list that included everything right, that we wanted to keep, and wrong, that we wanted to change about the old Cooper House," King said, the AWC also deciding to hire architect Rick Gilliland for the project. "We wanted a building to hold both large and small meetings, with a good kitchen and dining room," she said. And then the fundraising began in earnest. "We wanted a building that was traditional that would never go out of style but still have memories of the Cooper House; for example the patio have columns," King said "Wanted something that would look as nice 30 years from now as now."

The AWC was able, in the process, to increase its membership to 700 while also obtaining 501(c)3 nonprofit status and finding many donors that kept costs down.

"Roofing was contributed by the North Texas Roofing Contractors Association and other donated shingles," King said. "Contractor Barton Thompson became our champion among many champions."

The building was occupied in September of 2002 at a cost of about $1.2 million, though King estimates the building would have cost more than $2 million or more if not for so many contributors. The AWC members proudly burned the mortgage note in 2004, becoming debt free in the process and emerging from a potential tragedy as a much larger club with more than 700 members serving a wide range of interests.

"AWC members give thousands of hours in community service each year in addition to monetary considerations," current president Jan Simon said. "We will continue to provide support for many philanthropic causes throughout the Arlington community. For example, one of our favorite projects is the scholarship program which benefits AISD seniors in all seven high schools as well as mature women seeking to further their education at UT Arlington."

With a new home, expanded membership and a wide variety of interests the Arlington Woman's Club will be a critical ingredient in Arlington for many years to come, contributing to both the quality of life in the community and to the well-being and development of members.

One of the objectives of Arlington Woman's Club is to participate in philanthropic projects. Over the years, money has been raised with projects such as a booth at the community fair, tickets sales on small electrical appliances, cooking schools, flea markets, art shows, style shows, tour of homes, ticket sales to local amusement parks, auctions, bingo games, test market product tasting events, variety shows, raffles and large dinners. There is hardly a local nonprofit that has not benefited from the organization's help.

For example:

Year	Charity	Donation
1995-1996	Salvation Army Family Life Center	$7,127
1996-1997	Arlington Charities	$10,704
1997-1998	Arlington Women's Shelter	$12,000
1998-1999	Christmas Samaritans *	$200
1999-2000	Mission Arlington	$1,500
	Arlington Charities	$2,500
	Arlington Women's Shelter	$6,200
2000-2001	Meals on Wheels	$7,200
2001-2002	Arlington Night Shelter/Mission Arlington	$6,000
2002-2003	Arlington Night Shelter/AWC Foundation	$6,000
2003-2004	Arlington Night Shelter/Mission Arlington	$8,000
2004-2005	Arlington Charities	$7,500
2005-2006	Meals on Wheels	$15,000
2006-2007	HOPE Tutoring/AISD Families in Transition	$17,000
2007-2008	Mission Arlington	$24,025
2008-2009	Miracle Field of DFW	$28,463
	AWC Scholarship	$4,296
2009-2010	Arlington Urban Ministries	$30,000
	AWC Scholarship	$6,000
2010-2011	Arlington Charities	$17,975
	AWC Scholarship	$1,000
2011-2012	Grace After Fire**	$33,868

*The year the Cooper House burned.   **A program to assist women veterans.

In addition AWC operates its own scholarship program with a total of $17,500.00 given annually in scholarships. All seniors in Arlington high schools can submit an application to be considered for the $2,500 scholarship awarded to a student at their school.

Chapter 13 – Tipping Points

One revealing way to examine the history of any community is to look at it in the context of tipping points. These are trends, events or leadership—or a combination of the three—that accumulate to result in a sort of viral shift in direction, often abruptly. Not all tipping points are positive. Mining towns disappear because a copper vein runs out. Oil towns dry up when the geysers stop. Some Texas towns have literally disappeared because somebody in Austin decided that it was in the best interests of enhanced mobility to loop the main highway a few hundred yards and bypass the old downtown instead of running traffic through it.

Arlington, too, has had its tipping points. It's likely, for instance, that the city would never have existed in the first place if Texas and Pacific engineers hadn't decided in 1876 that they needed a stopping point midway between Dallas and Fort Worth. This was a tipping point of creation itself.

Consider these U.S. Census numbers for Arlington and the population trends they reflect:

Arlington Residents	
1920	3,031
1930	3,661
1940	4,240
1950	7,692
1960	*44,775*
1970	90,643
1980	160,113
1990	261,721
2000	332,969
2010	365,439

Note in particular the 1960 numbers in italics. What has essentially been a sleepy little Main Street Our Town kind of place with very modest population changes suddenly has a more than six-fold increase in a single decade. Genius is not required to deduce that a tipping point or tipping points have occurred. Further, the trend does not diminish over the next four decades.

What happened? First, recognize that the heralded baby boom that makes up today's senior citizens was just being born in the wake of hundreds of thousands of soldiers returning from World War II and starting families. And second, understand that while the trend for the first half of the 20th century was for the population to leave the farms and go to the big cities, from the 1950s on the migration was from the big cities to the suburbs, starting with the suburbs closest to urban centers. Millions of people wanted to live in places like Arlington that offered proximity to giant job markets in Fort Worth and Dallas, but also offered good schools and an easily acquired mortgage on a brick house with a lawn and a two-car garage with two cars in it. This was not inexpensive and there was a distinct possibility that Mom might also need to work to pay for all of it.

Arlington would certainly have grown, regardless of leadership, to some extent simply because of its mid-Metroplex location and the power of sociological trends, but as is so often the case, leadership matters. Arlington's leader through most of the 1950s and all the 1960s was the extremely pro-growth Tom Vandergriff. The mayor put out the welcome mat for virtually any kind of development, and he was both good at it and lucky. In later years there would be a modicum of deserved criticism for the architectural standards of both the single family and multi-family housing created in the era as well as what many considered to be an excess quantity of apartments. Too, there was an evolving proliferation of minimalist strip centers, many of which were difficult to sustain as the city spread outward and newer, glitzier strip centers cannibalized clients from the older centers. But the post-war population wanted affordable housing with a suburban lifestyle. And they wanted it now. Though Arlington certainly has and had a wealthier population, the city developed primarily as a middle class mix of blue and white collar suburbia awash in a sea of dollars flowing from stupendous development fueled by America's exodus to the burbs.

Vandergriff knew that cities take their shape based on the highest level of transportation and communication available. He was lucky that the Texas Turnpike, now I-30, went through Arlington in 1957 but he also worked hard to make it happen. And, in what turned out to be an absolutely remarkable bit of foresight, he also began working on the future route of Interstate 20, the presence of which increased the city's commuter accessibility and auto reliance while creating a concrete river of cash flow that continued through this era.

Most certainly the construction of a General Motors plant in Arlington in the early 1950s put the city on the map as both a place to live and work. GM was a major tipping point in itself, but its presence was not luck. Vandergriff and his father, W.T. "Hooker" Vandergriff, worked hard to make it happen. Six Flags Over Texas Amusement Park might well have been Angus Wynne's idea but it required city support, which in those days meant Vandergriff's support. Six Flags was another tipping point, not so much for its value as a tourism attraction, but because it made it possible for millions of young people to know where Arlington was. Later, when they had jobs and families and wanted their own suburban homes, the first place that would occur to many of them would be Arlington.

Many would come. Many would go. Many would stay. Even today Arlington has one of the most robust in-migration, out-migration patterns in the country, census data indicating that as much as half the city's population had another city address five years earlier. And though the city itself offers a plethora of economic opportunities, Arlington has more commuters leaving every work day for jobs outside the city than any municipality in the nation, the convenience of its location being a major factor in this trend.

Leadership frequently makes tipping points tip. Vandergriff's first attempts to attract a Major League Baseball team were ridiculed. Initially, his attempt to attract the troubled Washington Senators was considered a joke—in no way could a town of then barely 100,000 people expect to attract a major sports venue. But the Senators, renamed as the Texas Rangers, showed up with Ted Williams as manager, and suddenly suburban locations with easy access to urban populations became a national trend that continues today. Luck helps. But communities that are the most lucky inevitably have the best leadership. It matters. This cannot be overstated and in this Arlington has clearly been most lucky, not only with Vandergriff but with farsighted visionaries like another mayor, Richard Greene, who managed to salvage both the General Motors presence and to retain the Texas Rangers. Or Mayor Robert Cluck, who somehow pulled off the cheapest possible deal imaginable for the city to attract the most valuable sports franchise on the planet, the Dallas Cowboys.

Cars, faxes, texts, e-mail, satellite dishes and proximity to one of the world's largest international airports make it possible for a city to be built on a more expansive automobile scale than exists in more population-dense urban environments. Arlington was shaped in design and scale by the availability of affordable personal transportation during its period of creation and greatest growth. In terms of physical size, just under a hundred square miles, Arlington and Paris, France, are about the same, though Paris is multiple times more populous. For Arlington, one of the big issues of the future will be sustainability in an age when it is clear that fuel prices will continue to escalate, making a commuting lifestyle more costly.

Developing or finding new leadership is always a work in progress. It's not always easy as the following anecdote illustrates. Members of the first Leadership Arlington in 1980 were gathered at the city's Fielder Museum on a fall afternoon, their purpose being to determine what topics the leadership's subgroups would study and present over the course of the year. One such suggested subject was the city's history.

"That's not a good idea," one of the group said with what sounded like accurate rhetoric. "Arlington has no history."

223

Clearly one of the first tenets of leadership would be to know what one is talking about. But the remark—as disavowed by the pages illustrating this chapter—illustrated just how very quickly a sense of place and history can be lost, particularly in a city that has experienced such explosive growth over the last half century. In reality, Arlington is one of the oldest cities in the Metroplex and has an enormously colorful history resplendent with Indian tribes, pioneer battles, Old West gunfights, horse racing and other gambling (some legal and some not), train crashes, political clashes, population booms, demographic shifts, amusement attractions, boundary disputes, professional sports teams and a full measure of winners and losers in never-ending capitalistic struggles.

Beneath all that it has been a college town for more than a century, a reality that saturates the city with writers, artists, teachers, scientists and, of course, students. The city is a Mecca for both economic and intellectual opportunities and, as such, pulses with an energy that many communities would both relish and covet.

Despite its 366,000 population it remains a work in progress, which most urbanists would say is a good thing. Communities that persevere and prosper constantly remake themselves and have identities and brands that evolve with the marketplace and demographics. In an intuitive sort of way through a combination of leadership at the right time and perhaps a fortuitous location and some extraordinarily good fortune, Arlington's leaders and residents have generally been able to identify the forces pushing the future and make the most of them. Or, in some ways, work around the occasional setback.

What kind of setbacks? Donna Darovich's Arlington: Center Stage in the Metroplex, written in 1994, noted the pending arrival of Railtran. This was a commuter rail system that was to have been completed through Arlington by 2003, providing a mass transit link with Dallas, Fort Worth and DFW International, as well as with other Mid-Cities. That may happen someday but the progress toward that goal in 2011 was the same as 1994—talk and hand wringing but no action and certainly no funding. The billions of dollars that would be required along with extensive rerouting of the existing Texas and Pacific Railroad routes has proven to be enormously expensive to the extent that many transit experts say is very close to impossible. In fact, the city's voters continued to soundly defeat any attempt to implement mass transit in the city, preferring to stick with auto reliance. There are implications of this that will be expanded later in this chapter.

Likewise, the pending construction of the Superconducting Super Collider in Ellis County back in the 1990s was considered to be a virtual asset to Arlington when first announced. The primary link between the collider and DFW International would be through Arlington and Texas 360, which would result in an accelerated development of the roadway. Of equal importance was the fact that the collider would attract high level university researchers, many of whom would end up at UT Arlington and speed the university on its way to becoming a Tier I top-flight research university, a goal that is still being sought. Congress eventually killed the collider, and with it a vision for both Arlington and the region.

Though enrollment at UT Arlington today approaches 35,000, another setback for Arlington was creation of the University of Texas at Dallas. It was clearly a duplicative, expensive politically motivated addition to the system that was originally created as the Graduate Research Center of the Southwest and which evolved into UTD over time, gradually expanding its undergraduate offerings from upper class through all levels. Were it not for the presence of two competing universities within the same system it would not be a stretch for UT Arlington to have an enrollment of 50,000 today. As the saying goes, things are what they are, and Arlington long ago grew accustomed to the reality that it's a competitive world and no community wins them all.

But again, UT Arlington has been fortunate to have remarkable leadership. UTA's enrollment had grown to about 25,000 when UT Dallas began its expansion and for a while it seemed that there was a parallel between UTD's growth and UT Arlington's shrinking student body—and there probably was. Too, the presence in Arlington of a new Tarrant County College campus opening in 1995, offering two-year associate degree programs, clearly affected UTA's enrollment for a time. The arrival of Robert Witt as UTA's president reversed this downward trend, which has been dramatically accelerated by his successor, James Spaniolo. UTA has increased its enrollment to almost 35,000 in 2011 while the TCC campus is now approaching 15,000. Arlington has been a college town for more than a century, but the presence of 50,000 students and a faculty involved in all kinds of knowledge-expanding research represents an amenity and an appeal that few cities can match. Both UTA and TCC added classroom space in 2011 as UTA in particular transitioned from a commuter college to a more traditional on-campus residential community and moved toward the promise of developing into a Tier I research university. Thousands of students in proximity to downtown—and a new multipurpose center—promises to accelerate downtown redevelopment, perhaps morphing into the college town atmosphere that is so attractive to what urbanist Richard Florida describes as a "creative class" that is economically upscale and entrepreneurially active. Arlington is not an Austin nor a San Francisco, but those models are the long-term direction.

One of the advantages Arlington seems to have is that its ever-changing population and leadership doesn't discourage easily. No Super Collider? Make UTA a research institution and create the town's own technology incubator. No mass transit? Invest in better roads. Seven Seas fails? Convert the property to a highly successful convention center and hotel site. The town motto might well be "Keep on keeping on."

Over the years many Arlington studies have been conducted and many master plans outlined. These predict what kind of roads, water supplies, parks, libraries and other amenities will be needed for future populations. These studies often are criticized for having what many, at the time, considered overzealous predictions of growth to come. True enough, such studies do tend to be less than accurate in predictions but in an understated way. More often than not, Arlington outdistances projections and thus exceeds even optimistic expectations.

An advantage to a city built to automobile scale is that it has more flexibility to change itself. It can continue to expand outward, as Arlington is doing with development north of the Trinity River that will eventually increase population by 20,000, or it can expand skyward with high density mixed use development. The city has such a concept on the drawing board now, modestly termed the Lamar-Collins Overlay. Essentially the idea is to allow owners of aging apartment complexes to redevelop as mixed-use high rises with stores and offices below and apartments and condos above. It'll be necessary to check in ten or twenty years from now to determine if the market likes this idea. Arlington, locked into its not-quite hundred square mile area, cannot annex more territory. It is surrounded by other municipalities. Its growth must take place within existing boundaries.

Brian Cotter in his architecture master's thesis on Arlington described the city as "exopolitan," essentially seeing the community as neither suburban nor urban, having "the horizontal character of suburbia with all of its urban conveniences but without the vertical nature of the urban environment." In short, Arlington ends up being more populous than a St. Louis or a Pittsburgh, but doesn't have the impressive skylines of those cities. Cotter believes this hybrid community lifestyle is relatively new to America, though with a familiar constant.

"It is a form of community dependent upon the automobile," he said. "This new form of community is still maturing, leaving many to ponder just what will it be when it grows up. Whatever it will become, today's exopolitan community has developed as an outgrowth of late twentieth century America, and it is the community of choice over both urban and suburban cities."

Given the increasing population of projects like the Huffines Communities development in north Arlington and the likelihood of more dense multi-family development, it is a foregone conclusion that Arlington will exceed a population of 400,000, probably by the next census. But growth beyond that will be considerably slowed unless more inclination is shown toward vertical construction—going skyward as the town runs out of prairie on which to sprawl.

Arlington is not an island. It affects and is in turn affected by events and trends around it, some from its nearby neighbors of Fort Worth and Dallas and some from the halls of government in Austin or Washington, D.C. And it feels the ripples, of course, coming from Wall Street.

The city's very first master plan in 1953 put a premium on developing a concept urbanologists now call "multiple urban service centers." This means that instead of a downtown providing the majority of commercial services, there are many centers that provide these services, some being small strip centers and some not so small, like the Parks Mall of Arlington or the Arlington Highlands. A purist might insist that this is a somewhat wasteful system, but for most people this kind of proximity to services and amenities produces considerable savings in both energy expenditures and time. It is less costly and time consuming to drive a few blocks to a bank, restaurant or movie than to journey to a crowded downtown miles away, there to be gouged by expensive parking costs. People intuitively know what is most efficient for them, which is probably a major reason that Arlington has grown so rapidly. One downside is that once-prosperous shopping areas with names like Park Plaza or Town North have declined over the years and become something of a liability.

Other minuses? In some respects the every-family-with-their-own-lawn within a sea of cul-de-sacs, often without sidewalks, is isolating and can be wasteful. It can discourage a sense of community and certainly makes it more difficult to walk and bike. The idea that every American has the ability to go anywhere they want and to bring two tons of rolling steel with them is costly and has some undesirable environmental consequences, including wasteful consumption of limited resources like fossil fuels and air pollution problems.

Nevertheless, if there is such a thing as a safe prediction to be made about Arlington 20 or 30 years from now, it will be that it will not have fully embraced the central city format and that the auto will still be a central feature, albeit in much smaller vehicles with electric or alternate fuel power. It also does not seem unreasonable to expect that there will be some proliferation of high-rise living and that the presence of those denser populations will in themselves encourage commercial activity in their proximity.

Darovich, in her 1995 "Center Stage" tome, did not anticipate the arrival of the Dallas Cowboys, but she did predict that the area around the Entertainment District would include riverwalk entertainment and other visitor attractions. Indeed, the city did have plans for exactly such a complex but it stalled because of a national recession. But the idea remains valid and inevitable. In 1995 the city was having tourism traffic of about six million a year. That number is now closer to ten million, an irresistible opportunity for what eventually will be more development in the city's Entertainment District. The Cowboys stadium has already hosted a Super Bowl, a Cotton Bowl, a National Basketball Association All-Star Game and multiple big-name concerts. The Rangers in both 2010 and 2011 ended up in the World Series. The city's Municipal Airport on the I-20 corridor has boomed with private jet traffic.

At the same time the city's downtown area, which struggled for decades, has experienced and continues to experience a kind of renaissance. Long-time downtown advocate and Councilwoman Lana Wolff calls the downtown "everybody's neighborhood." It is not a traditional downtown, instead featuring a blend of restaurants ranging from Babe's Chicken and the ever-eclectic Gilligan's to Flying Fish, with more on the way.

In 1991 Theatre Arlington moved into the former Keir Lumber property at the corner of Main and West streets near the Arlington Municipal Building. The renovated building now boasts a 199-seat theater and is the sixth largest community theater in the Southwest. A revamped Arlington Music Hall hosts country Western one night, the Arlington Symphonic the next, and is bookended by two popular restaurants.

Arlington Country Music Revue

The gemstone of downtown Arlington is now the Levitt Pavilion, which provides 50 free concerts a year while hosting many other events. Many of the Levitt concerts have been so well attended that nearby streets must be blocked off to accommodate listeners. The impact of UTA's 6,500 seat special events center, which opened downtown in 2012, will likely be significant, as will be the expected arrival of more than a thousand university student housing units along the downtown corridor, the last of which will open in late 2012.

Downtown exists within the virtual shadow of the Cowboys' stadium and the economic ripple effect has already been substantial. Whether this activity will spread to nearby Division Street—the old Bankhead Highway—or east on Abram Street, old State Highway 1, is yet to be determined. The trend, however, is encouraging. Perhaps only a city like Arlington would first abandon the idea of a traditional downtown, only to reconsider and begin creating another model completely, that being a sort of eclectic "communiversity" mix of university activities, restaurants, night life and theater.

If there is a constant in Arlington's sense of place from 1900 on, it is that the city has long considered itself to be a place where people come as day or weekend tourists. It's an idea that surfaces repeatedly: healing minerals of crystal springs, horse and dog racing, gambling in the town's old casino, Six Flags, Hurricane Harbor, conventions, Major League Baseball, Dallas Cowboys, sports events and concerts. One consequence of an auto reliant city that also hosts 10 million or so visitors annually, punctuated by sports venues or concerts that have been known to attract 100,000 fans, is that the city's traffic can be monumental depending on events. Throw in a Rangers game on the same day of a Cowboys game, on the same day that Six Flags has a big concert attraction—like the Beach Boys—and getting around in some parts of the city or using major highways can be distinctly cumbersome. In this, however, Arlington's residents are somewhat akin to people who live on the coast and intuitively understand oceanic tides and surges. Resident Arlington drivers automatically compensate for changing traffic conditions, making use of their superior knowledge of city roadways and avoiding high traffic areas before they become an obstacle. Visitors, however, do not usually have this advantage.

In time the vision for the downtown area is for it to evolve into a less brash version of an Austin-style Sixth Street that can be enjoyed by locals, university students and visitors alike. Too, San Antonio's River Walk is the source of considerable envy virtually everywhere in Texas and there is a recurring wish to create a similar enclave of shops, restaurant and clubs around the small lake and large granite sculptures of Caelum Moor within the Entertainment District. That both of these visions will occur is likely, though no doubt there will be considerable tweaking along the way.

Perhaps not surprising in a city that loves to spread out, Arlington also relishes the outdoors. The most impressive example of this is the sprawling, 1,300-acre River Legacy Parks that spreads along the Trinity River from city limit to city limit. The hope is that eventually a trail system between Dallas and Fort Worth will link with Arlington in the middle. Though accessible, River Legacy retains its 300-year-old oaks, through which visitors hike, jog, skate and bike. Despite its urban location the park is home to hawks and doves. Whooping cranes occasionally make stops on migration flights. Bobcats, coyotes and foxes are common. Urban children who might not otherwise see a real oak forest learn about the realities of a wild environment at the park's Nature Center. Kayakers and canoeists use the park's canoe livery to launch their craft and journey through a waterway that in some sections will appear much as the Caddos saw it in their own canoes.

Another linear park, one developing along Johnson Creek as it meanders through the heart of the city, has not been developing as rapidly as its River Legacy cousin but nevertheless offers great promise for the future, connecting as it does with several existing parks—including Vandergriff, Meadowbrook and Richard Greene parks—and the university. A future Johnson Creek linear park, in tandem with an expanding bike path and bike lane system, will offer not only a respite from the steel and asphalt of the city but a way to walk or bike through miles of the city without venturing on a roadway.

Much of what happens in Arlington in the future will depend on the inclinations and ambitions of its residents, the demographic makeup of which has changed dramatically over the past 50 years. Half a century ago, very close to 90 percent of the population would have been non-Hispanic Caucasians. Today, both the school district and the overall city have majority minority populations, the city in 2011 being about 40 percent Caucasian, slightly more than 27 percent Hispanic—the fastest growing group—and almost 14 percent African American. The city also had about 25,000 Vietnamese residents, with other nationalities making up the remainder of the population. The Vietnamese population ranked among the 15 largest in the nation. Almost 19 percent of the city's residents were foreign born. Arlington has been evolving into an extremely diverse city.

As early as 2000 it had become evident that a great deal of entrepreneurial activity in the city—particularly the central east side—was originating from Hispanic or Vietnamese business activity. Residents overall were younger than the state or county average, the median age being 31.2. The population was relatively affluent, with a median household income of about $56,000 annually. About 58 percent of the city's households were home buyers, the remainder home or apartment renters, though the trend has been more in favor of an increasing percentage of home renters. The city is so reflective of what most of the U.S. will eventually look like that Arlington is often used as a test market for new products. Whether the increasingly diverse residents will bond as a community or disperse into a more culturally fragmented population has yet to be determined, but thus far Arlington has managed to avoid the classic racial divides that ultimately boil down to a contest of wills between haves and have-nots. At some point the demographic mix distinctly has the potential to create yet more directional tipping points in areas ranging from political emphasis to allocation of social service resources.

What is also clear about the city is that it is gradually changing its focus to a more controlled growth and a higher quality growth, in tandem with increased emphasis on redevelopment like that occurring in the downtown area. Standards for both single family and multi-family construction have been upgraded, as well as commercial construction and signage. More stringent landscaping standards have been implemented, often to the consternation of developers who preferred more leeway in architecture and less costly impact fees. This is a municipal philosophy that—if discipline can be maintained—will eventually transform the city into a greener, quieter and certainly more scenic community. But it may also slow growth to a degree unknown.

A critical unknown is what Arlington will eventually do about the mass transit issue, which in some respects is as much about social engineering as mobility. The reality is that it is difficult—perhaps impossible—to create more dense population and business environments without a mass transit accommodation, with only auto service. Arlington voters have not embraced this reality and even if they were suddenly to change that attitude, the traditional funds that would be used are not available. A form of financing that does not currently exist would have to be created, not an easy task. While Arlington has taken auto reliance as far as it can likely go, that may be something that voters are happy to simply live with for at least another decade.

Certainly a big part of Arlington's future is to be self-restorative, adaptive—presumably including mass transit someday, some way—and movement toward a strategy of growth for a better quality of life as opposed to growth for growth's sake. Arlington is no longer a new city, but it has enormous quality of life assets that include three institutions of higher education, a premium location in the Metroplex, amusement and entertainment attractions of enviable dimensions and a knack for showing up with the right leadership just when tipping points arrive. The city's potential remains dynamic. It can still grow horizontally for a while, vertically forever and has the potential to expand its reputation as a good place to live and prosper. It can rebuild its downtown in a new and unique way, expand its Entertainment District and add new businesses and homes. It can nourish the technology and research created by its university, and create new businesses not only for Arlington but for the region and Texas. There will be challenges, new tipping points and a few failures but more successes. That's been the history of the town—find a way and keep on keeping on—since its creation.

About the Artist

Irene Glass, a native of Missouri, garnered her first art award at the ripe old age of 10. It was the portent of many to come. Galleries in Hawaii, New York and Texas have shown her work. Irene became a military wife when she married Isaac Glass and their travels afforded her the opportunity to study with notable artists from the New England coast to the mid-west, the Louisiana Bayou and Hawaii.

Studying with outstanding artists brought Irene a greater level of understanding of all media, though she says oil and watercolor are her favorites. Her teachers and mentors include Al Bradbury, Joyce Clark, Lau Chun, Susan Taylor and Barbara Engles in Hawaii, Robert Wood and Barbara Nechis in New York, Christopher Schenk in California, Victor Armstrong in Texas and Virginia Cobb in New Mexico.

While living in Honolulu, she was intrigued with the ethnic features of the Hawaiian people, as well as studying and painting the ocean. For five years, she had a gallery in Eaton Square on Waikiki Beach.

A 35-year resident of Dalworthington Gardens, Irene said creating the historical illustrations for "Caddos, Cowboys and Cotton" was a labor of love in many ways. She has a keen interest in history and has long been a fan of Carter's writing. As a long-time member of the philanthropic Arlington Woman's Club, participating in a project which will benefit the club makes it even more rewarding.

Irene is involved in numerous art associations and has taught classes in oil for 10 years. She currently operates a studio from the Glass home in Arlington. She and Isaac have four adult children.

Acknowledgments

Participants

Our thanks to the Arlington Woman's Club members who participated in the production, promotion and sale of this book.

Beth Anderson	Jo Johnston	Virginia Ramsey
D'Ann Besley	Mary Belle Keller	Ethel Reeder
Loesje Blumberg	Vicki King	Dorothy Rencurrel
Pat Burdette	Beverly Koch	Connie Ruff
Barbara Castano	Laura Lace	Kristina Rumans
Sue Stevens Durbec	Mary Laport	Shirley Simpson
Beverly Feuling	Martha Martin	Martha Stallings
Theresa Gilmore	Sue Mattlage	Lucy Thompson
Irene Glass	Ruth McKee	Carol Tieman
Catherine Hopkins	Carrol Nokes	Laurie Tittle
Medora Houston	Lynda Nunez	Kim Werdman
Cheryl Illingworth	Josie Lu O'Quinn	Jean Widmann

Donors

The Arlington Woman's Club thanks the donors whose generosity made this book possible.

AWC Art & Design Department
AWC Bible Department
AWC Book Review Department
AWC Creative Living Department
AWC Garden & Gourmet Department
AWC Literature Study Department
AWC Mah Jongg Department
AWC Thursday Bridge Department
AWC Travel Department: in Honor of Irene Glass
AWC Tuesday Bridge Department
Arlington Woman's Club Board: 2009-2010
Frost Bank
Miranda Bateham: in Memory of Dale & Ricky Bateham
Martha Bird

Donors (continued)

Loesje Blumberg

Kathleen Brennan

Judy Buie

Cherry Coffman

Shirley T. Cole: in Memory of Bill E. Cole

Leon and Cissy Conley

Bob and Anita Copeland

Paula Cox: in Memory of Louise Shallcross

Charlene Dorsey

Charles and Joan Duke

Judith Evans-Presley

Bernice H. Gildner

Bill and Theresa Gilmore

Catherine Hopkins

Medora Houston

Jane Johnson

Jo Johnston

Richard and Vicki King

Laura Lace

Pat and Ann LaPosta

Ruth McKee

James and Carrol Nokes

Lynda Ray Nunez

Erin Rayfield: in Memory of Ethel Roy Brown

Dorothy Rencurrel

Martha Stallings: AWC President 2009-2011

Nancy York: in Memory of Anne Sanderson

Index